W9-AHU-983

THE HOT L BALTIMORE

By the same author

THE RIMERS OF ELDRITCH AND OTHER PLAYS

THE GINGHAM DOG

LEMON SKY

THE HOT L BALTIMORE

THE MOUND BUILDERS

5TH OF JULY

BALM IN GILEAD

TALLEY'S FOLLY

THE HOT L BALTIMORE

A play by
Lanford Wilson

A MERMAID DRAMABOOK

HILL and WANG   NEW YORK

A DIVISION OF FARRAR, STRAUS AND GIROUX

HMWQ
C₁

For Marshall Mason

THE HOT L BALTIMORE was first presented on February 4, 1973, at the Circle Theatre, 2307 Broadway, New York City. Producers Kermit Bloomgarden and Roger Ailes transferred the Circle Theatre Company production to the Circle-in-the-Square Theatre, where it reopened on March 22, 1973, with the following cast:

BILL LEWIS	*Judd Hirsch*
GIRL	*Trish Hawkins*
MILLIE	*Helen Stenborg*
MRS. BELLOTTI	*Henrietta Bagley*
APRIL GREEN	*Conchata Ferrell*
MR. MORSE	*Rob Thirkield*
JACKIE	*Mari Gorman*
JAMIE	*Zane Lasky*
MR. KATZ	*Antony Tenuta*
SUZY	*Stephanie Gordon*
SUZY'S JOHN	*Burke Pearson*
PAUL GRANGER III	*Jonathan Hogan*
MRS. OXENHAM	*Louise Clay*
CAB DRIVER	*Peter Tripp*
DELIVERY BOY	*Marcial Gonzales*

The play was directed by Marshall Mason, with sets by Ronald Radice, costumes by Dina Costa, and sound by Charles London.

The author expresses his thanks to the John I. Guggenheim Foundation for their support during the writing of this play.

THE HOT L BALTIMORE

The People

MR. KATZ

> The hotel manager. Thirty-five, balding a little but hiding it. Firm and wary and at times more than a little weary. Dark, in an inexpensive dark suit. A baritone

MRS. OXENHAM

> The day desk clerk–phone operator. Forty-five and firm; quick-speaking with no commerce

BILL LEWIS

> The night clerk. Thirty, large-featured, well-built in a beefy way, a handsome but not aggressive face. He covers his difficulty in communicating his feelings for the Girl with a kind of clumsy, friendly bluster. Baritone

PAUL GRANGER III

> A student, twenty. Blond, angular, and taut. His tenor voice is constrained by anxiety, he speaks and moves sporadically. Clear, lightly tanned complexion

MRS. BELLOTTI

> The mother of a former tenant, fifty-five. Round and thin-voiced; complains to get her way, she is a whining fighter. Neatly but not expensively dressed. A sigher

The Residents:

MR. MORSE

> Seventy, craggy, with a high, cracking voice. Morse moves slowly, with great energy and a sense of outrage

MILLIE

> A retired waitress, sixty-eight, with good carriage and a lovely voice. Elegance marred by an egocentric spiritualism

THE GIRL

> A call girl, nineteen. Light, blond, maddeningly curi-

ous; a romantic enthusiasm and a youthful ebullience, which is perhaps unconsciously exaggerated for its appeal in her trade

APRIL GREEN

A prostitute, over thirty. A large and soft pragmatist with a mellow alto laugh and a beautiful face

SUZY

A prostitute, thirty. She is hopelessly romantic and hard as nails. A mezzo

JACKIE

Twenty-four. Jeans, boots, her name written on the back of her denim jacket. Her manner, voice, and stance are those of a young stevedore. To her humiliation, she is, under the manner, both femininely vulnerable and pretty

JAMIE

Jackie's brother. Pale, small, and wiry. A little slow (one suspects browbeaten). Alert but not quick. Always listening to his sister. Nineteen

CAB DRIVER

DELIVERY BOY

SUZY'S JOHN

The Scene

Once there was a railroad and the neighborhood of the railroad terminals bloomed (boomed) with gracious hotels.

The Hotel Baltimore, built in the late nineteenth century, remodeled during the Art Deco last stand of the railroads, is a five-story establishment intended to be an elegant and restful haven. Its history has mirrored the rails' decline. The marble stairs and floors, the carved wood paneling have aged as neglected ivory ages, into a dull gold. The Hotel Baltimore is scheduled for demolition.

The theater, evanescent itself, and for all we do perhaps itself disappearing here, seems the ideal place for the representation of the impermanence of our architecture.

The lobby is represented by three areas that rise as the remains of a building already largely demolished: the Front Desk, the lounge, and the stairway.

Much of the action of the play is in the area behind the Front Desk. It should be open to the audience so we can follow the routine of the staff. Above this inner sanctum is a Rivera-style mural depicting the railroad's progress westward. Against the mural are stacked dozens of record books, boxes of files and letters. A broken TV is used as a table for paperbacks, a hotplate, and a radio. There is a card table; folding chairs where the hookers congregate; the usual switchboard (which should be practical); pigeonholes; and a sweeping desk that faces the lounge.

The lounge: a sofa and three or four chairs, none original to the hotel, are all re-covered in plastic fabric. There is a table large enough to set up a checkerboard. From the lounge the marble stairway rises and curves, leading off to one side.

There could be an elevator with a barricade across the doors. There is a door to a broom closet and the skeletal indication of the front door.

Over the center of the lobby is a non-working and almost

unseen bronze chandelier that serves as the source of power, via two extension cords, for the tinny radio and the office hotplate.

About the radio: the play is designed to incorporate music popular during production. The music plays in the theater before the acts, and as the lights dim, the sound fades into the radio on stage. At the end of the acts the radio music builds again, moving into the house. The first and third acts should end with a positive song with an upbeat, a song that one has heard in passing a dozen times but never listened to closely.

The time is a recent Memorial Day.

Act One

(PAUL GRANGER III *is asleep in a chair.* BILL *and* GIRL *are behind the desk; he is at the switchboard, she is sitting beside, watching the operation. Six lines are plugged into the board. A radio is just audible.*)

BILL
(*Into the mouthpiece.*)
It's seven o'clock. (*He disconnects one line.*) It's seven o'clock. (*He disconnects another.*)

GIRL
How do you do that? You plug everybody in at once, then just keep ringing until everybody answers, huh?

BILL
It's seven o'clock. (*Starts to disconnect the line.*) I don't know; I ain't been out, I got no idea.

GIRL
(*Impulsively into the phone.*)
Miserable. Terrible; it's raining and cold and—

BILL

(*Quickly disconnecting the line.*)

Don't do that. I told you, you can't do that if you're gonna sit back here.

GIRL

I want to find out what you're doing all the time.

BILL

You see why I don't have time to talk in the morning— (*Into the phone*) It's seven o'clock.

GIRL

I just answer the—

BILL

You don't answer, you ask questions. (*Ringing.*) Come on.

GIRL

It helps me get awake.

BILL

It doesn't help me any when I'm trying to—

GIRL

—When you wake up, don't you like a pleasant little—

BILL

(*Into the phone.*)

It's seven o'clock. Seven o'clock. (*Leaving the switchboard, turning off the radio.*) When I wake up, I get up.

GIRL

(*Taking up the call sheet.*)

Six different people having to get up at seven o'clock. I'd hate it.

(BILL *looks at her disapprovingly, then notices something on the stairs.*)

4

BILL
Who's there? Who's up on the—

MILLIE
(*Overlapping*)
Good morning, Billy; don't let me frighten you. (*She starts a slow descent into the light.*)

BILL
Morning, Millie.

MILLIE
(*To herself*)
I don't know why it should tire me going down the stairs. I believe my body's metabolism can't get it through its head that I'm in retirement. You'd think after six months I'd be able to sleep past six-thirty; but I can't even manage to get back to sleep in the morning.

BILL
(*Overlapping from "head"— Ringing.*)
Son of a bitch.

GIRL
Who's that? Maybe they didn't get in till late last night.

BILL
No, he's like that every morning. Same thing every morning. (*To* MILLIE—*who has reached the desk*)
You see what they're doing to the Pioneer? I drive by.

GIRL
That was such a beautiful place! Why do they tear everything down?

MILLIE
(*She takes a morning paper and goes to the sofa.*)
No, no, what would I care now?

BILL

They really built that old place; they're having a hell of a time getting it down.

(*Behind* GIRL's *back*) That's not the only building going under the ball, you know.

(*Indicating this hotel.*)

MILLIE

So I hear. Well . . .

GIRL

(*Overlapping "well"*)
Where do you live?

BILL

(*To* MILLIE)
Don't you want to—

GIRL

Where do you live? You said you drive by the Pioneer.

BILL

Uptown; don't poke me.

GIRL

Who do you live with? Are you married?

BILL

Come on! (*Turning to the switchboard; disconnecting the last line.*) It's seven o'clock.

GIRL

What are you doing? He didn't answer.

BILL

I'm giving up on him. What's the matter, Millie, kinda hate to see it go?

MILLIE

No, I have no feelings about it either way. They couldn't

afford the staff to keep it up any more. I long ago gave up being sentimental about losing propositions.

GIRL
Don't; I'm just going to get depressed. I really hate it that nobody cares about any— This used to be the most exclusive medium-sized hotel anywhere on the Eastern Seaboard line. This place was built—

BILL
How'd you suddenly get onto talking about—

GIRL
—in eighteen hundred and something.

BILL
What's this place got to do with the Pioneer?

GIRL
Oh, dummy. I can recognize a picture of my own hotel when it's on the front page of the newspaper.

BILL
Yeah, when was that?

GIRL
They used a picture from its grand opening.

MILLIE
I didn't realize it was this place, but I don't suppose I've looked at the building, really, in years.

GIRL
Oh, it looks just like it used to, only dirty.

BILL
(*As* MRS. BELLOTTI *enters*)
That's some news, huh?

MRS. BELLOTTI
(*At the desk, to* BILL)
Excuse me, is Mr. Katz in?

GIRL
He comes in at seven-thirty.

BILL
(*To the* GIRL)
Just never— No, he comes in—ain't in yet.

MRS. BELLOTTI
I don't think I've talked to you; I'm Mrs. Bellotti. Horse
Bellotti's mother. Mr. Katz is gonna give him another
chance, ain't he? He ain't gonna kick him out, is he?
(*As she starts to come right into the office,* BILL *jumps at her,
leaving the board.*)

BILL
Here, you can't come back here. Don't come back here. That
gate ain't supposed to be left open.

MRS. BELLOTTI
(*Overlapping*)
I can talk from here, this is fine; you'll talk to him, to Mr.
Katz, won't you? You look like a nice young man. 'Cause I
don't know what his daddy and me are going to do if he
don't—

BILL
(*Cutting in*)
—I don't know nothin' about it. I got nothin' to do with it.

GIRL
(*Answering the phone.*)
Hotel Baltimore, good morning.

8

BILL
(*Returning to the chair, shooing her out.*)
He'll do what he wants to about it. Come on.

GIRL
I'll connect you.

MRS. BELLOTTI
Only he can't kick him out. I don't want him coming back
to some strange place somewhere else. Does he want more
money? Is that what it is? Does he want more money? 'Cause
Horse's bill is always paid full on the first of every week;
he's never been a day late with it. Is that what he wants?

BILL
(*Ignoring her. He has replugged a line. Ringing.*)
Damnit.

GIRL
You gonna try him again? (*Reaching.*) Let me ring him.

BILL
No! Come on—make us a—why don't you make us a cup of
tea?

GIRL
Millie, you want a cup of tea?

MILLIE
(*Looking up from the paper.*)
No, thank you, Martha.

GIRL
(*Wincing.*)
Ohhh, it's not Martha any more; I hate it.

MILLIE
I thought you had decided to settle on Martha.

9

GIRL

No! I mean I did, but I hate it. Where's the mailman? It's after—

MILLIE

On Memorial—

GIRL

Oh, I can't bear days when there's no mail delivery. Weekdays. What's this stuff?

BILL

That's something for you to do; those go in the boxes.

GIRL

(*Taking up the stack of thirty-five envelopes.*)
Terrific. Oh, no. You know what it is? It's our— Oh, that's horrible, I certainly am not. It's our things. Eviction notices. "Newgate Development and Management"—

MILLIE

Let me see.

GIRL

Oxenham can do it; she'll love it. Just tell me how long a notice they're giving us. (*Her attention now is on the pigeonholes.*) Can you imagine people not picking up their mail? How can they bear it? Two-twelve. Must be a salesman. (*Takes four or five letters from the box.*) Baltimore, Baltimore. Boring. Denver. Something Idaho.
(*To* BILL)
What does that say?

BILL

Don't take people's mail out of their—

GIRL

I'm gonna put it back—what does that say?

BILL
If you can't read it, I can't.

GIRL
(*Categorizing it.*)
Some sloppy town in Idaho. Washington, D.C. I've been over every inch of Idaho twice. Sugar beets, potatoes, and cows. Denver is gorgeous. (*Going on—another box.*)

BILL
Don't mix those up.

GIRL
I'm not. Don't bother me. Annapolis—nowhere. Baltimore. New York, Baltimore. Here's one I don't know. Franklin, Louisiana. No idea. Millie, you ever heard of Franklin, Louisiana?

MILLIE
Down on the Gulf, I believe.

GIRL
In the heel or the toe? You know.

MILLIE
Well. The ball of the foot.

GIRL
Around Saint Martinville?

MILLIE
South of there; right on the Gulf.

GIRL
Right. (*Disposes of it.*) Swamp City. No wonder.
(*As* MRS. BELLOTTI *starts to move away, ignored*)
You come back at seven-thirty—quarter to eight, and he'll be here.

MRS. BELLOTTI

(*Immediately drawn back.*)

Has he said anything? To you? 'Cause I don't think he really has it in for Horse. He just doesn't understand him. He shouldn't have gone in, really. And he's only been in for five months, so you know it wasn't anything bad; he's a nice boy. He's just different. He's been to a psychiatrist and he gave him a complete examination and he said there wasn't anything wrong with David mentally; he's just shy. I tell him —Horse . . . you should meet someone. He's too adult to live with us. He's thirty-six. He and his dad don't get along. I tell him he has to *try* to meet people—to meet a girl, and he says how would I do that? And I don't know what to tell him . . .

GIRL

(*As* BILL *disconnects the plug*)

You giving up on him again?

BILL

He'll call down to Oxenham at ten o'clock, mad as the devil.

MRS. BELLOTTI

You think he'll let him stay?

BILL

Mr. Katz is in by eight o'clock, you come back then.

MRS. BELLOTTI

I just came by on my way to— I'm supposed to be home with Frank 'cause he's on morphine and God knows what condition he might be in. We're all the way out in— You think he'll be to work by eight o'clock? Is there a place where I can get a cup of coffee or something? Or I'll just sit here and wait till he comes in if he's going—

BILL
There's a place on the corner's got real good coffee.
(GIRL *punches him—it has notoriously bad coffee.*)

MRS. BELLOTTI
That's what I'll do; 'cause I can't afford to go all the way home and come back. And I can't talk to him on the phone 'cause he won't come to—(*Fades off and listens.*)

BILL
That Pioneer used to be a pretty slick place, did it?

MILLIE
(*Putting the notice in her purse.*)
Oh, yes . . . thirty years ago or more, people found it a pleasant enough place to spend their money.

BILL
President Taft used to go there? .

MILLIE
President Coolidge. The father of the "constructive economy"! I served him quite often. He always sat his party in my station.
(MRS. BELLOTTI *wanders off and out.*)

GIRL
Does she have a son that lives here?

BILL
I don't know *who* she was. You can't come back here if you don't close that gate.
(*To* MILLIE)
He a pretty good tipper, was he?

MILLIE
President Coolidge? Not at all.

BILL

No?

MILLIE

No tip at all. He didn't pay and he didn't tip. I think the pleasure was supposed to be mine.

BILL

You're a hard one, Millie.

MILLIE

(*Pleased.*)

No, no . . . not really.

GIRL

Did it have ghosts? I mean it had been there so long . . . probably not, though, huh? In a restaurant?

MILLIE

Oh, yes. There were a number of *spirits*. One or two who never left the dining room. They were almost as much a fixture as I was. One particularly.

BILL

Didn't nobody sit on him?

MILLIE

Oh, *she* never sat. She was very shy; she just stood about, near the doorway. We often saw her when we were cleaning up.

GIRL

Who was she?

MILLIE

Someone who liked the restaurant, it would seem.

GIRL

Are there ghosts here? There are, aren't there?

MILLIE
They don't like to—

GIRL
I *knew* it! I *knew* it!

MILLIE
They don't like to be talked about; it would only upset them.

GIRL
Well, Lord knows I'm not going to upset them! Could you tell my fortune? Because I believe in— Oh! Listen!
(*In the beat of silence there is the echo of a train, not far off.*)
Oh, no! (*In a rage of disappointment.*) That's the Silver Star! Oh, damn! Doesn't that just make you want to *cry?* How can they do that!?

BILL
I think she's got the schedules and bells and whistles all memoriz—

GIRL
(*Angry.*)
There's no schedule involved in it. I don't think they have schedules any more. Silver Star is due in at four-nineteen; she's more than three damn hours late. I get so mad at them for not running on time. I mean it's their own damn schedule, I don't know why they can't keep to it. They're just miserable. The service is so bad and hateful, and the porters and conductors, you just can't believe it isn't deliberate. I think they're being run by the airlines.
(*To* MILLIE)
Do you have stock in the railroads? Could you do something? Write somebody?

15

MILLIE

Oh, no; I don't have much stock. Certainly not in the railroads. I can't imagine anyone with any business sense just now—

GIRL

Where will they go?

MILLIE

Who?

GIRL

The ghosts? When they tear the hotel down? What'll happen to them?

MILLIE

Oh . . . they'll stay around for a while wondering what's become of everything. Then they'll wander off with people. They form attachments.

BILL

(*As the board lights up*)

Now what does he want? (*Phone.*) Yeah? Front desk.

APRIL

(*Entering; from off.*)

All right, all right, what's the story this time? Last week it was a plumber in the basement; two weeks before that he said the boiler was busted; the time before that, the coldest fuckin' day of the year, he's got some excuse so stupid I can't even remember it.

BILL

(*Phone.*)

You put in a call for seven o'clock. It's seven o'clock. (*Disconnects.*) Whadda you want, April?

APRIL

(*Overlapping*)

Seven o'clock? Who you tellin'—it's no goddamned seven o'clock—it's not been light more than—

GIRL

I told you two weeks ago; spring ahead fall back.

APRIL

What kind of monkey language is that supposed to—

BILL

—Don't you listen to the radio or read a—

APRIL

—The fuckin' daylight savings. (*Turning to go.*) Fall back on my ass; it's too scratchin' much. I don't know what anyone expects—

BILL

(*Overlapping*)

It's been almost a month, April; you oughtta be used to it by now.

APRIL

(*Returning.*)

Hey, come on, I gotta get to sleep—whatta you gonna do about the water?

BILL

What's wrong with it?

GIRL

It's cold.

APRIL

No. Last night it was cold. Tonight it's cold—and it's orange.

BILL

They're probably workin' on the pipes.

APRIL

Yeah, well, I'm gonna work on somebody's pipes. (*Hikes her leg up on his chair, looking and scratching.*) Things aren't wicked enough around here with—

BILL

(*Overlapping exchange*)

—Come on, I'm not in your way, am I? What are you doing?—

APRIL

—I'm not bothering you—

BILL

—What have you got your leg up in the air—

APRIL

—You're not going to see anything—

BILL

(*Getting up.*)

—What are you getting on me?—

APRIL

—Whadda you think, I'm lousy? (*Shaking her hair on him.*) Waaaaaaa!

BILL

Come on, whatta you doing? What the hell's wrong with you?

APRIL

(*Laughing.*)

You really are an ass acher, you know it?

BILL
Whadda you want, April?

APRIL
Don't start with me. What I want, this hotel don't offer.

BILL
I'm trying to work here.

APRIL
What are you doing about the water?
(*He starts to speak.*)
Tell me you just work here.

BILL
(*Beat.*)
What're you coming down here in your nightgown?

APRIL
What nightgown? This is a silk—Dacron kimono. This is a perfectly respectable garment. Whadda you think, I'm trying to turn you on? You're not my type.

BILL
I didn't know you had a type.

APRIL
(*Abstracted*)
Yeah . . . well . . . I've got several types. Give me a cigarette. (*Helping herself; chuckling.*) A guy—yesterday—said, you sure smoke an awful lot—asked did I smoke in bed—I said . . . try me.
(*Laughs.*)

GIRL
That's dangerous. Smoking in bed.

BILL
(*Phone.*)
Front desk. Yeah. Hold on. Hand me that book.

APRIL
Morning, Millie.

GIRL
What number?

MILLIE
Good morning. I don't
know whether to say good
morning to you or good
night.

BILL
Two-eighteen. Just see if
he's up on his bill.

GIRL
What does he pay—weekly?

BILL
Let me see it.

APRIL
Say good night to me and I'll curl up right here on the floor.

GIRL
He paid half and then the rest yesterday.

BILL
(*Into the phone*)
Yeah. What was that number?
(*He writes it down*— GIRL *begins to dial before he is finished.*)
O.K.

APRIL
Thanks for the butt. Put a note in my hole I don't want to
be rung till after four o'clock.

GIRL
Is that an eight or a zero?

BILL
Come on—three-eight-six-oh.

GIRL
(*To* APRIL)
Don't forget to turn your clock up.

APRIL
I don't keep clocks. Clocks and dogs. My clock's outside my window on the front of the terminal. Says a quarter after five. Twenty-four hours a day. (*Laughing.*) I figger that's a good enough time for just about anything. (*Laughing.*) Guy came up to me last week—couldn't think of anything to say —said—"Uh, uh, excuse me, you don't happen to know what time it is, do you?" I said, Sure, it's a quarter after five. The son of a bitch was so surprised he looked at his goddamned watch. (*Laughs.*)

GIRL
(*Pause.*)
What time was—

APRIL
I don't want to hear it. Whatever you're going to say. You're a real bring-down, you know it? I'd give a hundred bucks for her hair; I wouldn't turn a nickel for her brain.

GIRL
No, I got the joke, I just wondered what—

APRIL
Listen, don't listen to me. Kids now are a different breed. If I was sixteen I'd be just as— How old are you?

GIRL
Nineteen.

APRIL
Nineteen. Jesus. If I was nineteen and looked like that—

BILL
And know what you know now.

APRIL
Fuck what I know now. Give me the rest of it—I'll learn. You want to know the sad truth? If I looked like that I wouldn't have to know what I know now.

GIRL
Did you ever take a ride on a—

APRIL
What? On a what? (*Beat.*) Probably I did.

GIRL
Nothing. I don't want to know what you'd say.

APRIL
Yeah, well, I got that problem. Listen, I'm going to bed before I get bitter. (*Takes another cigarette.*) You tell Katz I'm after his balls if he ain't got hot water when I get up.

MR. MORSE
(*Overlapping a word or two—entering*)
I have a complaint. Who's here? I have a complaint.

BILL
What's yours, Mr. Morse?

APRIL
Lay it on us, Mr. Morse.

GIRL
(*Simultaneous*)
Morning, Mr. Morse.

MORSE
(*Simultaneous*)
Listen to me.

BILL
Yeah.

MORSE
Listen to me!

BILL
I hear you.

MORSE
I'm going to hold the hotel responsible.

BILL
Why's that?

MORSE
Listen to my voice.

BILL
I hear you, Mr. Morse.

MORSE
Listen to my voice. I can't afford to get a cold and I'm getting one.

BILL
That your complaint?
(APRIL *laughs.*)

MORSE
My window won't close. It's swelled tight and there is an inch crack that won't close all the way.

APRIL
That's just advancing age, Mr. Morse.

GIRL
You got the same complaint, huh?

APRIL

I wouldn't go that far.

JACKIE

(*Entering, followed by*
JAMIE, *who goes immedi-*
ately to the sofa and sits.)
(*To* APRIL)
Listen, April, could I ask
you a personal thing—one
thing.

APRIL

I'm just trying to get to
bed, lady.

JACKIE

Sure, right, that's cool.
(*To* GIRL)
Bitch of a day, ain't it.
(*To* BILL)
Listen, Hal—er uh—Bill:
I pay my bill, right? I mean,
you know the way I do
things; like I haven't caused
any problems around here
—nothing like that—right?
That's not the way I op-
erate . . .

MORSE

I put a towel into the crack
and I wrapped up my chest
and neck, and it still didn't
help. And I—I am going to
hold the hotel responsible,
I got very little sleep.
You're responsible if something isn't done. Because
there's *dampness* in my
room. And if I'm taken to
the hospital, I'm going to
hold the hotel responsible
for the bill!

BILL

(*Overlapping*)
Hold it, I can't hear you both at once. I'll send someone
up to close it for you, Mr. Morse. It just needs some weight
behind it.

(*To* JACKIE)
What is it now?

JACKIE

You're still not calling me Jackie. You know better than that. I like everything out front. First name.

BILL

I can't remember everybody's name here.

JACKIE
I been a friend here, right? To you and these people. We don't trespass on people's feelings. Me and my brother don't bother anybody. I mean, we been here what? Nearly a month: you got the rent receipts there. We been here, we ain't complainers. That ain't the way we live. We don't have people up to our rooms. (*As* BILL *is showing no interest*) Second thought, skip it, I'll wait for Katz.

MR. MORSE
(*Slight retard.*)
That window should be repaired. If it just needed to be closed, I could close it myself. I'm capable of closing my own window. You send a man up there with hammer and nails and tools. I'd do it myself if I had the proper tools. And I'm coming down with a cold. With a severe cold.

APRIL

What's the matter, Mr. Morse, lose your tools?

MORSE

There's *dampness* in my *room*.

BILL

I'll send someone up to close it.

JACKIE

Sure ain't gettin' any warmer, is it? It's the East Coast. It's bad for your lungs to live this close to the ocean. It's bad for you.

MORSE

It's bad.

JACKIE

Your throat and chest.

GIRL

I didn't know that.

MORSE

And my health is on the point of breaking.

JACKIE

What's he got? You got a problem with your window? I'll shut it down for you. Give me your keys; it's no trouble.

BILL

No, no— (*He starts to get up as the phone buzzes.*)

JACKIE

People got to help one another, don't they?

MORSE

(*Taking out his keys.*)

I'm coming down with a severe cold and I'm going to hold this hotel responsible. And my neck is getting stiff.

JACKIE	BILL
(*Taking the keys.*)	(*Phone.*)
I believe in helping each other where you can. It just needs somebody to put a	Front desk. Yeah. What's that? Nine, three? (*Writing.*) Is that in Baltimore?

few calories into it. It's no
problem.
(*She goes upstairs.*)

    (*Starts to dial, notices* JACKIE.)

GIRL

Probably just needs a good push.

BILL

(*Phone.*)
Hold it. (*Yelling after* JACKIE.) Come on! (*To phone*) Hold it.
(*To* JACKIE) You! What the hell's her name? Don't go up there. Hey! (*Sotto voce*) Son of a bitch. (*Back to phone.*) Yeah?

MORSE

You have no right to object if that young man wants to help me.

APRIL

Mr. Morse, you gotta throw away the mustard plaster and take something worthwhile to bed with you.
(*He mutters and heads to the lounge.*)
You want to volunteer, Lilac?

BILL

She's a little young for him, don't you think?

APRIL

That's all right; by the time he gets it up, she'll be old enough.

BILL

(*Phone.*)
Four-three-oh-seven. Yeah. Been pretty quiet. No, she paid—

MORSE

There's somebody sleeping in my chair.

27

APRIL

They eat your porridge you're shit out of luck, ain't you, baby?

GIRL

He's waiting to see Mr. Katz.
(*To* APRIL)
You want a cup of tea?

APRIL

Whatta you got? I'd kill for a chicken broth.

BILL

Come on! (*Turning to phone.*) Him too, the both 'em paid: receipts in the book. Naw. Naw, it's been pretty quiet. O.K. (*Disconnects as* JAMIE *starts for the stairs.*)
Here! Where you going?

JAMIE

(*Freezing.*)
I wasn't going any place.

BILL

You just stay down here till she comes back down here. Katz'll be in in a few minutes.

MORSE

Here. Boy. Where's our board?
(JAMIE *shrugs, hangdog; mumbles.*)
Either you want to play or you don't want to play.

JAMIE

I'll play.
(*They look for the board.*)

GIRL

(*To* MORSE)
Did you know they were going to tear down the—

MORSE
What?

GIRL
(*Louder.*)
They're tearing down the hotel; they're gonna tear down this building.

MORSE
Good!

GIRL
Listen!

APRIL
What?
(*A not too distant train bell.*)

GIRL
It's pullin' out.

APRIL
You got the ears of a bat.

GIRL
Holy—it's three hours late now; by the time it gets to Miami, it'll be six hours overdue again.

BILL
She knows what she's talking about; she's been on all of 'em.

APRIL
Trains give me a pain.

GIRL
I used to live right by a railroad track. I never waved to a single person who didn't wave back to me.

APRIL

The tracks I can take or leave.

GIRL

—If you saw something important to you neglected—like that. They've let the roadbeds go to hell. You have to close your eyes on a train. Or look out the window. That's still beautiful; some of it. In the country.

MORSE

Where's the board? Bill?

APRIL

The one time I remember taking—

BILL

What? Be quiet a minute. What?

MORSE

Somebody took the checkerboard.

BILL

I got it back here; you left it out. Nobody put it away last night.
(*He hands it to the* GIRL, *who takes it to the lounge where* MR. MORSE *and* JAMIE *begin setting it up.*)

GIRL

Can I watch?
(*Nothing.*)

MILLIE

When I was a girl I used to ride back and forth between Columbia and Baton Rouge on the Gulf Raider.

GIRL

I don't think I know that one.

MILLIE

Oh, it's not running any more, I'm sure. It was a wonderfully elegant coach. They had a shower . . . they had—

GIRL
They had a shower?

APRIL
On a train?

MILLIE
Oh, yes—I'd seen it a number of times. I decided once to take a shower before I retired. I walked the full length of the train in my bathrobe and slippers and shower cap, carrying a towel and my soap. Through the dining cars with everyone having dinner. I'm sure I'm the only person who ever took advantage of the shower. It was a marvelous train, very modern—Art Deco then—chrome and steel. Quite the thing.

GIRL
They used to keep on schedule, didn't they?

MILLIE
Well, I know the service was excellent; and one went from one wonderful terminal to another—

GIRL
—Only you should see them now—

MILLIE
—But the schedules? Oh . . . they (*Drifting away*) may have. Maybe not during the war when so many servicemen rode the trains; it seems they used to. It didn't matter so much if you came in a few hours late. I don't know. I've always thought of myself as a bit outside society; I never seem to understand what other people expect.

APRIL
I took a train once, and let me tell you I—

GIRL

—I don't want to hear it. Whatever you did. Whatever it was, I don't want to know.

APRIL

I was eight years old. What could I do?

GIRL

I don't care. Something. You probably got raped. I don't want to hear it.

APRIL

I most certainly did not get raped! I have never been raped! I'd say there was little likelihood of me *ever* getting raped.

MORSE

There's one missing. There's a red checker missing.
(*As* KATZ *enters, walking straight to the office*)
Somebody didn't put them back properly.

GIRL

Good morning.

KATZ

(*Taking off his coat.*)
Morning. Who's the boy in the lobby?

BILL

Guy says he wants to see you.

KATZ

How long's he been there?

GIRL

Since about four.

BILL

Came in about four; said he'd wait.

MORSE
(*Coming to desk.*)
There's a red checker missing from that box.

KATZ
—We've had complaints about your singing in the lobby again.

MORSE
(*Furious.*)
Who? Who said anything? I have already complied with those complaints. I ought to do those exercises in my room but I moved to this lobby because people sleep during the day. Those exercises are important to my health. Prescribed by my physician and I—

KATZ
I'm just telling you—you create a scene.

MORSE
Who said it? I have a right to know who said it.

APRIL
Mr. Morse, for a seventy-year-old man with his voice going, you got a healthy set of pipes when you need 'em, ain't you?

MORSE
That singing is necessary to—

APRIL
Honey, I don't mind the singing; I just wish you'd learn the words to the song.

MORSE
—I have a right!—

APRIL
All right, Katz. Speaking of pipes—you know the hot water in this hotel?

KATZ
Yeah?

APRIL
Well, I hate to be the one to tell you, but I think it's coming down with hepatitis.

BILL
Damnit! Here, cover the board. I almost forgot that girl went up to Morse's room.

KATZ
What girl?

BILL
That girl with the brother. She—
(JACKIE *comes down before he can leave the desk area.*)
Don't go up to rooms here. Like that.

MORSE
Those exercises are important to my health.

JACKIE
His window was stuck. I helped him out. He ought to sleep with it open anyway; you can't talk to him about it.
(*To* KATZ)
Look at this here, now. I been waiting for you to get in. Did you see that Belair out there?

KATZ
I don't know, no.

JACKIE
Parked right in front of the door.

KATZ
I didn't see it.

JACKIE

Well, that's my wheels. I bought it two weeks ago. Paid cash. That's the way I like to do things—

JACKIE	MORSE
Only I can't put it on the road till I get plates. See, I was driving it, but a cop stopped me; 'cause the plates on it don't belong to it.	(*Yelling back hoarsely.*) People . . . are not . . . considerate . . . of other . . . people . . . is my complaint! (*Sits at checkerboard.*)

KATZ

Stopped for what?

JACKIE

For the plates. The plates was expired. Some pig. You're not listening to me—

KATZ

—What do you want? Say what you want. You and your brother both. You've always got angles—angles— I don't have the—
(*Shuts up as she rides over him.*)

JACKIE

(*Cued by "brother both"*)
Could I have just three minutes of your time? That's all I'm asking, just three minutes of your time. See, the title's clear; it's clear and paid for cash. I got the inspection sticker —never mind what I had to go through—but I can't put it on the road without the plates and the thing is you got to get your insurance to get your plates. I didn't know anything about that 'cause I ain't had wheels in my name before.

KATZ

I don't know nothing about it; I don't drive a car.

JACKIE

(*Overlapping some*)

That's what they told me. I just kept it out of the yard
'cause I told them I was getting the plates. And I went
around—never mind where I had to go—what I have to
have is Ten, Twenty, and Five. That's what they call it.
Ten thousand for a single injury; twenty thousand for a
multiple, and five for damages. Collision you don't have to
have.

APRIL

I don't know why people have cars.

JACKIE

(*With a glance to her but no pause.*)

—'Course every place has a different price: right there
you know what kind of a racket they're running. Like the
ones you've heard of are way-out-of-sight, off-the-wall clip
joints. But the minimum I need for Ten, Twenty, and Five
is $165; that's all it'd take to—

KATZ

I can't help you with it—

JACKIE

What with? With what? I'm not asking you for money. I'm
not a borrower. I don't take a penny from nobody I don't
know. I wouldn't have to pay the hundred, I'd just need
sixty-five down and quarterly, if I hadn't got canned from
the pet shop— Only I wasn't canned. I saw what was coming and walked out on them. The pansy manager was trying to get me fired so his little friend could have my job.
I hit him with a birdcage and walked out on the bastard.
He kept live snakes as pets, if you want to know the sort
of person he was. Let them run loose in the shop at night.

GIRL

You hit him with a birdcage?

JACKIE

He was mincing down the aisle with this stack of bird-cages, he made a crack I won't repeat; and I took one of 'em and slapped it alongside his head.

APRIL

I don't know why but I believe that.

JACKIE

He called me up, tried to tell me I owed him for a myna bird. There wasn't no goddamned myna bird in that cage. Where you going?—I'm trying to tell you something.

KATZ

I don't know what you're talking about. I'm working here. I got no time.

JACKIE
(As SUZY *and a client enter*)
I'm telling you. If you'd stop interrupting. I need a friend. I'm in a bind. Straight out—that's the way I deal: I need a friend. That's what I'm saying; I need a pal.

KATZ
(To SUZY's JOHN, *who precedes her upstairs*)
Here! Here! Where you going? Has he got a room?

SUZY

I hope you don't mean—

KATZ

—You! Hey, come down here!

SUZY

—What are you doing? Are you crazy? He's a friend of mine! We're going to have a little drink.

37

(KATZ *retires.*)
If you please. I'd appreciate it if you'd cool down. A little bit here.

SUZY'S JOHN
(*Whispered.*)
Come on, Christ.

SUZY
I'm trying to clear up a misunderstanding, here.
(*To* KATZ)
I don't like to be prosecuted.

APRIL
You don't like what?

SUZY
(*Laughing with her.*)
First thing you ever heard me say I didn't like, huh?
(*Laughs.*)
How about this crummy *weather?*

APRIL
(*Laughing.*)
Those are the ugliest shoes I ever saw!
(*Both laugh.*)

JACKIE
What's funny about them?

SUZY
She gave me those shoes—

SUZY AND APRIL
Last night!
(*They laugh.*)

SUZY
You're three-nineteen.

JACKIE
We're tryin' to transact some business here.

SUZY
Ain't ya? Three-nineteen?

JACKIE
Yeah; me and my brother.

SUZY
I'm four-nineteen. I'm right over you.

SUZY'S JOHN
(*A whisper.*)
You're on the fourth goddamned floor of a walk-up?

SUZY
I hope I don't keep you awake.

SUZY'S JOHN
Come on, would you?

JACKIE
You eat good food, you eat natural products, you don't have trouble sleeping.

SUZY
With the noise!

JACKIE
I never noticed no noise.

SUZY
Whadda you mean you never noticed no noise?

JACKIE
I never noticed no noise.

SUZY
(*Furious.*)
Well, what the hell, are you deaf?
(APRIL *laughs.*)
What the hell are you laughing at?

SUZY's JOHN
Come on, goddamnit. I ain't got all day. Get on with it.
(*Touches her lightly.*)

SUZY
Just don't assault me, if you please.

SUZY's JOHN
I said, I don't have all day. Come on, now, or forget it.

SUZY
(*To others*)
Are you going to allow me to be assaulted?

SUZY's JOHN
All right, then, forget it.

SUZY
I'm coming. Just don't rush me. These people are friends
of mine. Learn to live at a leisurely pace. You live longer.

GIRL
Did you know they're tearing down the hotel?

SUZY
Tonight?

GIRL
We're all going to have to move before long. It's been sold.

SUZY
What do you mean, move?

KATZ

Go on up—not now; everybody does. They're tearing it down. You'll have to find another place.

SUZY

When? What is this? Who said? I don't move for nobody. To hell with it; find another place, where? I got eleven-foot ceilings in my room. Where am I going to find something like that?

KATZ

What do you care what your ceilings are?

APRIL

If you spent as much time looking at the ceilings as she does, you'd care what they looked like.

GIRL

I wonder what's gonna be where my room is? I mean, in that space of air? That space will still be up there where I lived. We probably walk right under and right past the places where all kinds of things happened. A tepee or a log cabin might have stood right where I'm standing. Wonderful things might have happened right on this spot.

APRIL

Davy Crockett might have crapped on the stairs. Pocahontas might of got laid by—

SUZY

(Overlapping)

You're horrible! You have no human soul! I thought that was a beautiful thought.

APRIL

People who get her space are gonna wonder why it's so hot.

SUZY

People who get yours are gonna wonder why it stinks. I hope they do tear it down; this place is disgusting!
(*Pushing the john ahead of her.*)
I suppose you'll use this as an excuse not to fix the elevator.
(*Exits.*)

APRIL

(*To* SUZY'S JOHN)
Hey, keep your business out of her filthy mouth, up there!

KATZ

Every morning she's drunk and she acts up like that! (*Beat.*) People!
(*Pause.*)

JACKIE

So what I did was, I went to the bank. And they're willing to give me the money, even without the job, if I can get someone to co—

KATZ

(*Overlapping*)
No! No! Can't do it. I'm not in the business. The hotel won't do it and I won't do it personally. Not even if I knew you, and I don't know you.

JACKIE

(*Simultaneously*)
I'm not asking you for anything. It's not costing— I only want you to sign a paper. All I need is a signature. On a paper; your name on a paper.

KATZ
No. No. No.

JACKIE

(*Taking a pear from a paper sack, biting into it furiously.*)
Your fuckin' name on a fuckin' piece of paper.

KATZ

Watch your voice.

JACKIE

Forget it. Skip it. I don't need it. Just come out and look
at the car. Just see it—see if you—

KATZ

(*Re: a receipt—to* BILL)
What is this? Who signed this?

JACKIE

You got a head harder than a bull's dick, you know that?

KATZ

Go on, don't hang around here with that talk.

JACKIE

We're not bothering nobody.
(MRS. BELLOTTI *enters and crosses to desk.*)

KATZ

Eat outside.

JACKIE

Eat out, my ass! (*She goes to the lounge.*)

MRS. BELLOTTI

Excuse me, are you Mr. Katz? I expected an older man from
your voice on the telephone. It must be wonderful to have
a nice position like this at your age.
(APRIL *hoots.*)
Now, Mr. Katz, you're not gonna kick Horse out, are you?
I got a letter from him and he said he was really gonna try

hard this time. You're gonna give him one more chance, aren't you?

KATZ

No.

MRS. BELLOTTI
(*Contrite.*)
What'd he do?

KATZ

He's crazy. He don't make sense. He don't talk sense. He's crazy.

MRS. BELLOTTI

It's the alcohol, that's what it is. I've told him but he gets out, and he gets so keyed up and nervous and anxious he takes a drink and he can't stop. People don't know what he's really like, like I do.

KATZ
He steals things.

MRS. BELLOTTI
You won't let him come—

KATZ

No. You gotta pick up his things. I told you before.

MRS. BELLOTTI

How can I do that? I'll have to take a little bit at a time. His daddy can't help, he had his leg took off; he can't get outta the house; he's on morphine.

KATZ

Take 'em like you got to take 'em, but take 'em.

MRS. BELLOTTI
What'd he do?

KATZ

He's crazy. Last time I let him come back he stole the telephone outta his room. Tried to sell it back to the hotel.
Said there was no telephone in his room.

MRS. BELLOTTI

See. He didn't need the money either. He was making
money clammin'. We bought him the rake—he saved
eighty-five dollars and bought a boat, and then one day he
sells the boat to a guy downtown for ten dollars. He said
he wanted to sell something.
(*She wanders to the lounge by* JAMIE *and the* GIRL.)

GIRL

He won't let him come back?

MRS. BELLOTTI

(*Shakes her head.*)
And my husband lost his leg. Did you know that?
(*Both* JAMIE *and* GIRL *shake their heads.*)
He always had trouble with it. He was a diabetic and he's
had to watch what he eats for ten years. We thought he
was going to be all right; then he got a craving.

JAMIE

Does he drink?

MRS. BELLOTTI

Oh, no, the doctor won't let him touch it.
(JAMIE *nods.*)
But last summer he got a craving for fruit. He ate fruit all
summer and he got worse and worse and . . .

JAMIE

I thought fruit was healthy for you.

MRS. BELLOTTI

Not for a diabetic. With all that sugar.

(JAMIE *nods.*)

But he craved it. And he had to go to the hospital and they took off his leg.

JAMIE

(*Simultaneous with her*)

Took off his leg.

MRS. BELLOTTI

It was either that or—that was the alternative. And he just got home from the hospital a month ago, and if he sees Horse's things come into the house, I don't know what he'll do. He already sent the neighbor girl I got watching him to the store for apple juice. I came home and he'd drunk a gallon of it.

JAMIE

Our dad died of diabetes.

MRS. BELLOTTI

Isn't it a terrible thing?

JACKIE

Come here.

(JAMIE *goes to her.*)

MRS. BELLOTTI

I gotta get Horse's things.

(*After a beat she gets up with a sigh and goes to the desk.*)

JACKIE

What are you tellin' her?

JAMIE

She was telling me about her husband.

JACKIE
I heard what you said. You want me to leave you again?
Is that what you want?
(*He sulks.*)
You just mind your own business.
(*To* MILLIE)
He's a little mixed up.

MILLIE
I'm sure you'll straighten him out.

JACKIE
I hope that's a friendly remark.

JAMIE
She said her husband—

JACKIE
What have you been up to? Let me smell your breath.
(*He resists.*)
Let me smell your breath.
(*He does*)
Are you tryin' to kill yourself with those cigarettes? Is that
what you're doing? Where are they?

JAMIE
I just had one I found in the—

JACKIE
I don't want to know where you found it. Where's your
angelica stick? I told you to suck on—

JAMIE
It doesn't work.

JACKIE
(*Getting another.*)

47

That's because you're not sucking on it. You're not sucking it; you're chewing it. Suck it.
(*He resists.*)
Suck it.
(*As everyone turns*)
What the hell you looking at? Ain't you heard anybody say suck before?

MRS. BELLOTTI
(*Overlapping*)
Could I have Horse's keys? To get his things?
(*She gets them.*)

GIRL
It really doesn't make any difference 'cause we all have to move anyway. They're tearing down the whole building, so we all have to move.

MRS. BELLOTTI
It's just so difficult to find a place that'll take him . . .

GIRL
I know.
(MRS. BELLOTTI *goes upstairs.*)

BILL
Whadda you know; you don't even know him.

KATZ
He's crazy.

GIRL
Well, anybody named Horse. By his own mother.

APRIL
Guy last week said I reminded him of his mother. (*Laughs.*)
I— No, it's too dirty, I'm not gonna tell it.

48

BILL

I thought you were going to bed.

APRIL

(*Laughing.*)

I kicked him out. I said—I wasn't entertaining no mother
. . . (*Laughing.*) No, it's too dirty.

JACKIE

(*To* JAMIE)

Now what's wrong with you?

BILL

(*To* GIRL)

You been up the whole night, have you?

GIRL	JACKIE
I'm not sleepy any more; I think I had too much tea to sleep. (*Pause.*)	We'll get someone to sign it; you ain't worried about that, are you?

BILL

Don't worry about them; they ain't worth it.
(*Pause.*)

GIRL	JACKIE
I'm not; I just don't like to see people need things is all. (*Pause.*)	We put the car on the road, we won't stop till we hit Utah.

BILL

Don't you think you better go to bed?

GIRL	JACKIE
I will before long; I don't sleep so much. (*Pause.*)	What's wrong? We're gonna be all right. (*Pause.*)

49

You don't have to remind
me; I been up twenty-six
hours in a row.
(*Pause.*)
I just don't like to see
people . . . need things
is all.
(*Pause.*)

BILL
Everybody needs somethin',
babe.

GIRL
I just don't like to think
about it.

JACKIE
Whadda you mean?

JAMIE
We're not going.

BILL
Don't you want anything?

JACKIE
Don't talk so loud.

GIRL
Oh . . .

JAMIE
We're not going to Utah.

GIRL
I want everything.

You don't have to think
about it; I always come
through, don't I?
(*Pause.*)
We put the car on the road,
we won't stop till we hit
Utah.
(*Pause.*)
That's what you want, isn't
it?

JAMIE
We're not going to Utah.

JACKIE
Just shut up about it. I told you we'd go.

GIRL
For everybody.

JACKIE
They don't have to know our business.

GIRL
I want everyone to have everything. I really hate spring here. Spring is the messiest thing I ever heard of. Dribble, dribble, dribble for three months straight. The radio said it'd be warm today: it used to rain and then it'd be sunny. I mean, immediately. When I was a kid.

BILL
That was when you was a kid?

MR. MORSE
Your move.
(JAMIE *moves;* MR. MORSE *jumps him double.*)

GIRL
It almost never rained anyway. But when it did, just the next day all the cactus would bloom all over.

JACKIE
(*Almost a whisper.*)
Miss? You know that loan shop? What time do they open, do you think? Would they be open by eight o'clock?

MILLIE
(*Quite loud.*)
The pawnshop? I'd imagine a business like that, they would get an early start.

KATZ
(*Regarding the receipt.*)
Whose name is that?

JACKIE
The bloodsuckers.

BILL
(*After a glance at the book.*)
Martha? What'd you put here?

GIRL
Oh. That's "Lilac Lavender." Only I wasn't sure how to spell Lilac, so I kinda scrawled it. Whadda you think? (*Both turn back without comment.*)

JAMIE
(*Getting up from the game as the long cry of a train whistle echoes through the lobby.*)
I'm going to help that lady move her boy's stuff down.

BILL
Which one is that? Lilac?

GIRL
(*Moving to the lobby.*)
That's a freighter. I don't think they even stop here.

MORSE
Here! Where are you going?

JAMIE
I'll come back; I'm not finished.

MORSE
You can't get up in the middle of the game. If you leave the game, I win.

JAMIE
(*From the stairs*)
No, you don't.

MORSE
That's the way I play.

GIRL
(*Giving* PAUL *a gentle push.*)
Hey, you said you wanted to see Mr. Katz?

PAUL
(*Stirring.*)
Come on . . . (*Back asleep.*)

BILL
(*Phone.*)
Four-three-oh-seven. Yeah. Martha?

GIRL
No joke, Bill, I really hate that name.

BILL
That's who she asked for. Don't take your calls down here.

GIRL
O.K., O.K. (*On phone.*) Hello; hi, Veda.

APRIL
(*Over*)
You ever hear the one about the—

BILL
I don't want to hear it.

APRIL
What the hell kind of mood are you in?

BILL
I've had enough of your jokes for a morning.

KATZ

Don't sit back here; come on, there's a coffee shop on the corner.

GIRL

(*To* BILL)
Gotta pencil?
(*He gives her one.*)

APRIL

That's pretty good, honey, you get room service. I have to stand on the ever-loving corner.

BILL

Just knock it off.

APRIL

I wasn't talking to you, squirt.

BILL

Come on, get out—you aren't supposed to be behind here. This is private back here.

APRIL

You got a problem, don't take it out on me.

GIRL

Would you stop talking when I'm on the— I'll be there. (*Hangs up.*) That's pretty impolite!

BILL

You too, go on, get on out. You aren't supposed to be here.

GIRL

Mr. Katz said I could take calls here if I was down here instead of in my room.

BILL

Well, it's not my problem; I'm off.

MORSE
Where did he go to?

JACKIE
Just never mind.

APRIL
Where you gotta go?

GIRL
Not far; just up to the Haven Motel.

BILL
Far enough without any sleep.

GIRL
Would you stop being a daddy to me. You want to help, you can give me a lift.

BILL
I'm not giving you a lift; you can take a taxi; tell your john to pay for it.

GIRL
Thanks a lot.

BILL
It's not even eight o'clock in the morning; you're going out to turn a trick. You got to be out of your mind.

APRIL
When we gotta be out of here?

GIRL
You're really an ogre.

KATZ
One month, you gotta be out.

JACKIE
Whadda you mean, one month?

MILLIE

That's what's in the notice.

JACKIE

Let me see; where does it say that? You can't kick us out of here without a notice. Give me my mail. Did I get one?

MILLIE

(*Simultaneous*)

I was going to tell you, but it was a little surprising. I thought you could wait and find out for yourself.

GIRL

One month? Where is Bill going to work?

BILL

Just don't worry about me.

MORSE

Good! Serve you all right!

GIRL

Yeah?

JACKIE

Maybe you don't care where you go; I happen to have specific plans.

BILL

Yeah. You don't worry about me working and I won't worry about you sleeping.

MORSE

Right. I don't care. What do I care where you go. I'll be glad to get rid of the lot of you.

GIRL

Did you know we were going to all be out in the street in that short a time and didn't tell me or anything?

JACKIE

You dummy, you think you're going to stay here?

BILL

You're on the street now.

MORSE

I don't intend to divulge my plans to anyone here.

Just because I know some-
thing doesn't mean I'm at
liberty to tell it.

GIRL
You knew! You knew we
were going to have to go.
You are really an ogre!
You're terrible.

BILL
I'll bet you don't even know
what an ogre is.

GIRL
I certainly do; I sleep with
five or six every day.

BILL
I don't want to hear about
what you do.

GIRL
Well, it certainly isn't any
of your business. I don't
understand you at all—

BILL
—I don't care what you do
with your life—

GIRL
One minute you're friendly
and nice and the next
minute you're—

You aren't the only person
with plans.

JACKIE
(APRIL *and* KATZ *are cued
in now.*)
To hell with it. I don't
care. They can tear it down.
I'm taking my brother and
getting the hell out of here
anyway.

MORSE
Good. Nobody cares. We
don't care!

JACKIE
Tear it to hell!

MORSE
Tear it to hell! RIP IT DOWN!
(*He begins to unpack his
barbells.*)

JACKIE
I don't care if you tear it
down this week. Because I
don't intend to hang around
here. That's not the way I
am. I don't hang around
where the damn building's
coming down on my head.
Fuck it. I got enough sense
to get out when the gettin's
good. This place would fall

57

BILL

—I just wish you were old enough or mature enough to know what you're throwing away. I personally don't care a dang what—

GIRL

—as bad as my own daddy. Worse. Because he at least didn't care what I did. He didn't even care if I was a hooker as long as I kept him in enough money to buy beer. That's why I left, only you're worse than he is.

BILL

—you do with yourself or how many ogres you entertain in a day.

GIRL

I'll bet you don't even know what an ogre is!

down in another six months anyway!
(SUZY's JOHN *comes down the stairs, walks directly through the lobby and out the front door.*)

APRIL

(*Cued above with* JACKIE's *"To hell with it."*)
If I'm expected to get out of here before my month's rent runs out, I know somebody who's going to get a fat refund on her bill.

KATZ

Nobody is refunding anything. You stay through June. Nobody's paid past the month of June.

APRIL

Don't expect to see my tail . . .
(SUZY, *off, begins to wail.*)
till the first of June, daddy. Just let me tell you right now. I don't care if the pipes bust and the place is flooded to the third floor. (*She notices* SUZY *as she appears on the stairs.*)

SUZY

(*Off. Over* KATZ, APRIL, BILL, GIRL, JACKIE, *and* MR. MORSE. *Cued by* APRIL's *"Don't expect to see my tail . . ."*)

You bastard. What do you think you're doing. Come back here! YOU CHICKENSHIT!

(*She appears on the stairs wrapped in a towel and nothing else, wailing after the* JOHN. BILL *turns on the radio, furiously.*)

SUZY

Come back here, you fuckin' masochist. He beat me! Why didn't you stop him? He locked the door on me! He pushed me out of my door and locked the door on me! Police! Why aren't you doing something? What do we pay you for, you yellow crud? Yellow crud!

APRIL

What you doing with the towel, there, Suzy? (*She laughs.*)

SUZY

(*Each sentence makes* APRIL *laugh more.*)

What the hell are you laughing at? I'd like to see what you'd do. You shut up! You shut up! (*Slaps at her with the towel.*) You're

KATZ

Get upstairs. Get on, get out of the lobby. You can't come down here naked.

JACKIE

What the hell are you doing?

(MR. MORSE *begins to march up and down swinging the barbells.* KATZ *catches sight of him now.*)

KATZ

(*To* SUZY)

Suzy, get upstairs. I'm gonna call the cops on you. On all of you. They would as soon run your ass in again as look at you. Get up to your room. Go on or spend another night in the can; make your choice.

MORSE

(*Singing.*)

O sole mio; O sole mio;

59

THE HOT L BALTIMORE

disgusting! I'm calling the cops! I want to make a complaint! Against April Green! And against the management of this hotel! Scum!

PAUL
(*Waking. Cued by "disgusting."*)
What the hell is this? What the hell is going on here? This isn't a hotel; this is a goddamned flophouse! This is a flophouse!

SUZY
You're right; that's exactly what it is; it's a goddamned flophouse. This is a flop-house!

O sole mio—
(*Over and over as he marches on.*)

JACKIE
Get your ass back up those stairs. If my brother comes down and sees you like that, I'm going to take you apart. Who the hell do you think you are? I hope to hell they kick your ass out into the street!

KATZ
Get up to your room; what the hell is this? Don't listen to April. Come on. Get upstairs. April, you shut up; I've had it with you two.

JACKIE
(*Over; cued by* PAUL.)
Right! This is a goddamned flophouse. Exactly. A fuckin' flophouse!

(JAMIE *carries a box down the stairs, dropping it when he sees the naked* SUZY. *Staring with his mouth open. The box contains hotel soap, towels, washcloths, etc., and things stolen from the neighborhood shops. Nearly everyone on stage laughs as* JAMIE *gapes at* SUZY *and the lights fade. The music soars over their laughter.* CURTAIN.)

Act Two

(*Music from the house fades into the radio.* MRS. OXENHAM *snaps it off.*

Natural tableau: In the lounge MILLIE *sits reading a newspaper.* MR. MORSE *and* JAMIE *study a checkerboard. At the desk,* MR. KATZ *looks at an open receipt book;* PAUL *leans on the counter, watching him.* MRS. OXENHAM *studies a stack of laundry lists. Afternoon.*

JAMIE, *without moving, studying the board, sucks on a stick of herb candy. This is the only thing happening. Rhythmically: suck—pause. Suck—pause. Suck—pause. Suck—pause. Suck—pause. Suck.*)

PAUL
(*Finally. Belligerently, which is his nature.*)
Are you looking for it or are you doing something else?
(*Pause.* KATZ *writes something, frowns at book.* MRS. OXENHAM *turns a page.* JAMIE *sucks, moves.*)

MORSE
Huh!
(*He studies the board.*)
(MILLIE *looks up at them, smiles to herself, as she does most of the time, looks back to the paper.*)

PAUL
He left about a year ago, or a year and a half.

KATZ
I told you; he wasn't here. He was somewhere else.

PAUL
He was here. Is this the Hotel Baltimore? Is this 63 East Madison Street? Is this Baltimore? You have people who get mail here who don't live here?

KATZ
Ranger. No.

PAUL
Granger. G. Granger.

KATZ
No, nobody like that.

PAUL
Do you remember every—

KATZ
Ask Mrs. Oxenham; I don't know him.
(PAUL *looks at him. Takes in air, blows it out. Looks over toward* MRS. OXENHAM, *begins to move down the counter to her.* MR. MORSE *moves.*)

MRS. OXENHAM
(*Before he reaches her; suddenly busy.*)
I don't remember him.

PAUL
(*Rapid exchange here.*)
A little quiet guy; he'd be about sixty-eight or seventy; and he wears a little derby . . .

MRS. OXENHAM
(*Cutting in.*)
No, if he was here I'd remember him.

PAUL
—Not "if." He was here—for two years; he wasn't a transient—

MRS. OXENHAM
—I don't know anything about it—

PAUL
—Well, do you keep records? You keep rent receipts? Do I have to tell you what to do?

MRS. OXENHAM
—I can't take time to go through two years of room receipts looking for someone who never lived here.

PAUL
You don't have to go through them, I'll go through them. You don't have to squat.

MRS. OXENHAM
You don't have to use that—

PAUL
—I'll go through them if you're paralyzed, lady—

MRS. OXENHAM
—We're not going to turn our records over to—

PAUL
—Listen, I been here twelve hours, all I been getting is a shell game here; you people think you're the C.I.A.

MRS. OXENHAM
We're not at your beck and call. We're doing you a favor.

PAUL
I don't see you doing diddle.
(*She glares at him, but in a minute, as a martyr, takes down a stack of record books.*)

MORSE
(*Immediately. As* JAMIE *moves*)
You have to take your jumps.

JAMIE
I don't have to.

MRS. OXENHAM
What name was that?

PAUL
(*Beat.*)
Granger. Paul Granger. G-r-a-n-g-e-r! (*Beat.*) P-a-u-l.

MRS. OXENHAM
Sit down; if it's in here, I'll call you. (*Beat.*) When was he here?

PAUL
It's been more than a year—like a year and a half.
(*He waits a moment as she begins looking. Then turns.*)

MRS. OXENHAM
(*To his back*)
We're not a missing-persons bureau, you know.

PAUL
(*Sits in the lounge, disgusted. Looks around. Focuses on the checker game. Watches them a moment.*)
You play chess?

66

(MORSE *and* JAMIE *turn to look at him, then back to the board.* PAUL *looks away.*)

MILLIE
I've been sitting here reprimanding myself for being so unobservant. I was realizing that there are very few people living here whom I would remember a year after they left. They come and go with such a turnover . . . and if he wasn't obtrusive . . .

PAUL
He wasn't.

MILLIE
I was at work by seven-thirty and usually not back before six; where was he employed, do you know?

PAUL
He wasn't. He was retired.
(MILLIE *goes back to her paper.* PAUL *sulks and lights a cigarette, looks over to* MRS. OXENHAM. *He becomes aware that* JAMIE *is looking at him.* JAMIE *is trying to frame a request for a cigarette.*)
Whatta you gawkin' at?
(JAMIE *snaps back to the game. Sucks.* MORSE *moves.* MILLIE *has glanced up and back down. The switchboard buzzes. The* GIRL *enters, sees a message in her mailbox, goes directly to the office.*)

MRS. OXENHAM
Four-three-oh-seven. We don't do that. I don't know anything about it. Who's calling?
(*To* KATZ)
It's another antique dealer about the fixtures.

KATZ
Give them the number.

MRS. OXENHAM

Call Newgate Development: RA 6–3700.

(*Disconnects.*)

(MRS. BELLOTTI *comes in. She tries to gesture, "I'm going up-stairs to—" as* MR. KATZ *looks up and back down— She drops it and starts on up.*)

GIRL

(*Tosses message in wastebasket. To* KATZ)

You know what I've decided, puddin'? They're not going to fix the water or the elevator or anything, are they? They're trying to force us to leave. Aren't they?

KATZ

You got a month's notice; that's the legal notice.

GIRL

Yeah, but you don't expect anyone to live here a month with conditions like that.

MRS. OXENHAM

We've got a man workin' on the boiler right now. I called him as soon as I came in.

MORSE

(*Overlapping, cued by "boiler." The exchange starts low and personal and builds.*)

You can't move twice.

JAMIE

I'm not.

MORSE

You took your hand off it.

JAMIE

I did not.

MORSE
You moved your hand; take that back.

JAMIE
I did not!

MORSE
You did so, young man!

JAMIE
I was thinking.

MORSE
You're trying to cheat!

JAMIE
You're a liar!

(MORSE *takes* JAMIE's *checker from the board and throws it to the floor. Glares at him.* MILLIE *follows this exchange, looking from one to the other, just before the action.* PAUL *ignores it to the end or nearly* [beat]. JAMIE *takes a checker of* MR. MORSE's *and throws it on the floor. They glare* [beat]. MR. MORSE *takes a checker and throws it on the floor. Each further move is an affront. They glare.* JAMIE *getting hurt and belligerent;* MR. MORSE *angry and belligerent—*JAMIE *takes a checker and throws it to the floor* [beat]. MR. MORSE *takes the candy stick from* JAMIE's *mouth and throws it to the floor* [beat]. JAMIE *takes a pencil from* MR. MORSE's *pocket, breaks it in his hands, throws it on the floor.* MR. MORSE *stands.* JAMIE *stands.* MR. MORSE *takes up the board, spilling the checkers, and with difficulty tears it in two along the spine and throws it on the floor.* JAMIE *glares. Takes up the checker box, tears it in two, and throws it to the floor* [beat]. MR. MORSE *overturns* JAMIE's *chair. Now they grapple, slapping weakly at each other and making incoherent*

69

noises and grunts, two very weak individuals trying to do injury to each other. Injury would be impossible. When they struggle, MILLIE *stands to get away.*)

MR. KATZ
(*As* JAMIE *tears the box*)
Here, that doesn't belong to you; stop it. Both of you; sit down and act right or you can't stay down here. Come on! Both of you!

GIRL
(*Overlapping*)
Jamie. Shame on you. Come on, stop that, what are you doing; you two babies. Shame on you. Stop fighting. What are you doing?
(GIRL *reaches them as they separate.* MR. MORSE, *from humiliation, shuffles directly to the only door in sight.*)

KATZ
(*Also coming from behind the office.*)
Where are you going? Here, you can't go in there—

GIRL
Mr. Morse, come back and apologize; don't go in—
(*To* KATZ)
Oh, he isn't going to hurt anything. My God!
(MORSE *closes door as she reaches him.*)

KATZ
—Get him out of there.

GIRL
Mr. Morse, you can't go in there, that's the broom closet. (*Knocks.*) Mr. Morse? You're sitting in there on the slop sink, aren't you? With all those smelly mops. Mr. Morse, Jamie's sorry.

JAMIE
(*To her, joining her as* KATZ *picks up checkers*)
I am not!

GIRL
(*Grabbing him, putting her hand over his mouth. The contact of a girl confuses and amazes him as much as the situation.*)
He's sorry.

MORSE
(*Offstage.*)
No, he isn't.

GIRL
(*As* JAMIE *struggles to talk*)
What?

MORSE
(*Offstage.*)
He isn't sorry!

GIRL
You hurt him very badly.
(JAMIE *struggles to protest.*)

MORSE
(*Offstage. After a beat.*)
Where?

GIRL
You blacked his eye.
(JAMIE *gasps at the scope of the lie.*)
(*To* JAMIE)
Come here. I want to show you something.
(*As she gets her purse*)

JAMIE
What?

GIRL
(*Digging in her purse, getting out the mascara.*)
Something fun.

JAMIE
What?
(GIRL *spits on the mascara.*)
No. No.

GIRL
Hold him, Mr. Katz.
(KATZ, *returning to the desk, gestures, "I want nothing to do with any of you."*)
(*Hating it, protesting, struggling,* JAMIE *nevertheless lets her put the darkening around his eye.*)

JAMIE
No, no, it's— Don't, come on! Don't mark me up.

GIRL
(*Over*)
Mr. Morse, he's in pain! It's terrible; you ought to be ashamed of yourself, Mr. Morse.

JAMIE
(*The second she releases him.*)
Let me see.
(*She hands him the mirror.*)
(*Whining*)
No . . . He didn't do . . .
(MR. MORSE *opens the door.* GIRL *takes the mirror.* JAMIE *slaps his hand over his eye.*)

GIRL

Go on—show him, Jamie. Show him what a brute he is. Show him what an ogre he is.

(JAMIE *does, pouting as though it were real.*)

MORSE

Good. Good.

(JACKIE *enters.*)

(JAMIE *puts his hand back over his eye and goes to the lounge to pout.*)

JACKIE

(*Livid.*)

Is anyone here driving a blue Plymouth? Does anyone in this hotel belong to a blue Plaza 1970—

KATZ

(*Overlapping*)

What do I know, I don't know what kind—what are you coming in here; you're always upsetting people; accusing people.

JACKIE

(*Less excited.*)

—I just want to know 'cause I got a scratch on my left front fender about two feet long. People have no respect for other people's property. You just got to learn that and live with it. Let me use your pen.

(SUZY, *with stoic bearing, walks down the stairs in her most conservative clothes. As* KATZ *glances up, her head raises slightly and she walks evenly on.*)

Is today a Jewish holiday? What's happening today? I been to three different pawnshops; they're every one closed.

MILLIE

I think it's Memorial Day.

GIRL
It's Memorial Day today.

JACKIE
The whole damn city's closed up like a nun; *something's* going on. Is the Post Office closed?

GIRL
Oh, sure.

MORSE
Where's the checkerboard?

KATZ
No more checkers. You get too excited.

JACKIE
What happened? What's wrong with your eye? Who put that goop on you?
(GIRL *is saying Shhhh!*)

JAMIE
He did.

JACKIE
All right, what's going on?

GIRL
Mr. Morse hit him.

MORSE
(*Overlapping some*)
I hit him.

JACKIE
(*To* JAMIE)
You starting fights with people now?
(*To* MORSE)
Why don't you pick on somebody your own size?

MORSE
That boy is a hellion, and I taught him a lesson.

GIRL
We were just kidding around.

JACKIE
(*Spitting on a handkerchief.*)
Wipe that off your face.

GIRL
Shhhhhh!
(JAMIE *takes the handkerchief and sits.*)

MORSE
I hope you've all learned your lesson.

GIRL
You don't know your own strength, Mr. Morse.
(*To* JACKIE)
It was just a joke.

JACKIE
Well, I don't want people joking with Jamie; he's not in good health.

GIRL
We were just goofing.

JACKIE
(*Going to desk.*)
Well, I don't want you goofing with him.
(PAUL *starts to get up.* MRS. OXENHAM *gives him a stony look and opens the records.* GIRL *sees him.*)

GIRL
(*To* PAUL)
You're still here; I thought you'd be gone. Did you get a room?
(*Pause.*)

75

PAUL
I'm trying to get some information.

GIRL
Are you just in town?

PAUL
Yeah.

GIRL
Where from? (*Beat.*) How did you get here? Train? Hitch? Where's he from, Millie?

MILLIE
I'm sure if he wants you to know he'll tell you.

GIRL
Millie sees things, knows things, she sees ghosts and auras and things. And believes in things, like reincarnation and old Chinese religions like yoga—

MILLIE
I certainly do not. And yoga is something one practices, not something one believes in.

GIRL
Well, then you practice it.

MILLIE
I certainly don't practice yoga.

GIRL
Come on, you know what I mean—

MILLIE
I can't remember someone he'd like me to remember; I don't think he'll be much impressed.

GIRL
Who do you want?

PAUL

Are you one of the residents? How long have you been here?

GIRL

Lived here? Seven months. Before that I was everywhere; I'm from Arizona. Where are you from?
(PAUL *looks around.*)
I'll bet I've been there. I'll tell you the places I've been and you tell me if I name it. 'Cause when I left home I went every place, for almost six months. I didn't stop more than three days in any one—

PAUL

(*Getting up, going to the desk.*)
Are you looking for it?

MRS. OXENHAM

When I find something I'll tell you.

GIRL

(*Whispered, to* MILLIE)
Who's he looking for?

MILLIE

Ask him.

GIRL

Who're you looking for?

PAUL

My granddad. (*Sitting back down.*) You didn't know him. He probably left before you got here.

GIRL

Is he Mr. Morse? Mr. Morse, do you have grandchildren?
(MR. MORSE *turns to go.*)
You don't have to go.

KATZ
Stay out of that closet.

MORSE
(*Has actually swerved to the closet—now the stairs.*)
I'm going to my room!

JAMIE
Good. Good riddance.

JACKIE
(*From the desk*)
Just clam up over there.

KATZ
Come on, don't spread that stuff here.

JACKIE
I'm not bothering you. This is official.

KATZ
Go over there.

GIRL
Don't expect Mrs. Oxenham to help you. She's an ogre. She's not human. (*Distracted.*) Boy, this place. (*Looks around.*) I been up thirty-three hours. I'm not trying to find out your business, I just want to have a conversation. O.K., tell me if this is where you're from. Uh. Denver. Amarillo. Wichita. Oklahoma City. Salt Lake City. Fort Worth. Dallas. Houston. New Orleans. Mobile. Birmingham. Memphis. St. Louis —don't look down, I'm watching your eyes to see if you make a move when I say the right one. Kansas City. Omaha. Des Moines. San Francisco. Portland. Seattle. Spokane. Minneapolis. St. Paul. Milwaukee. Chicago. Indianapolis. Cincinnati. Columbus. Cleveland. Pittsburgh. Buffalo. Albany. Utica. Boston. New York. Providence. Atlanta. Tallahassee.

(PAUL *begins to smile.*)
Orlando. Tampa. Jacksonville. Daytona Beach. Palm
Beach. Fort Myers. Fort—Fort Lauderdale! Fort Lauder-
dale!

PAUL
(*Smiling.*)
No.

GIRL
Fort Myers.

PAUL
No.

GIRL
You smiled.

PAUL
I'm not from Fort Myers.

GIRL
Then where? St. Louis.

PAUL
No.

GIRL
'Cause that's when you looked away.

PAUL
You haven't been to those places.

GIRL
I certainly have.

JAMIE
You've been to Salt Lake City?

79

GIRL

I been to every state in the Union. Some of them three times.

PAUL

That'd cost about—

GIRL

Yeah, I sold cookies. Come on, you're trying to distract me. Los Angeles.

PAUL

No.

GIRL

Bakersfield.

PAUL

No.

MILLIE

Louisville.

(*He looks at her—reaches for the paper; she hands it to him.*)

PAUL

Where is it?

(*He hands it back to her; she finds the item and returns the paper to* PAUL.)

GIRL

(*Overlapping the action. Amazed.*)
Is that *right?* I would have *said* that.

JAMIE

Come on.

GIRL

(*To* JAMIE)
I would. I've been there. I went from Knoxville to Chat-

tanooga to Nashville to Evansville to Louisville to Cinci— (*She notices something is wrong.*) What?
(PAUL *hands her the paper. She glances down, then up.*)
Your name's Paul? (*Back to the item.*) The third. What's St. Clemens?

PAUL
(*Pause.*)
It's a work farm.

GIRL
What'd you get busted for?

PAUL
Selling grass.

GIRL
They give you two years—

PAUL
Shhh!

MILLIE
(*Whisper. At the same time.*)
Now, not so—

GIRL
—for selling grass?

PAUL
You're supposed to drink sour-mash whiskey. You're not supposed to be selling grass. I was an example. They like their students drunk, they don't like them—

GIRL
You were in *school* and they gave you—

PAUL
Shh—come on.

GIRL

In college? (*Pause.*) I'm impressed. I didn't even make it past junior year in high school. I hated it.

PAUL

Don't let it bother you. It's just a way to keep the kids off the street.

MILLIE

It doesn't seem to be working, does it?

GIRL

(*As* PAUL *smiles at* MILLIE'*s joke and she smiles back*)
Boy, I was terrible in high school. I failed every subject except geography. I was pretty good in history but I was a genius in geography. Naturally, I'd be good in something I couldn't possibly use. Actually, I do use it, though. Like when a john is shy or weird or something, I can ask him where he's from and get him talking. I don't think that's what Mrs. Whitmore had in mind when she taught us geography. (*Beat.*) You're looking for your granddad? Did he just disappear? While you were—"working"? Will they look for you?

PAUL
No. Do you mind?

GIRL
Did you just sneak off?

KATZ
(*To* JACKIE)
What are you doing? What are you spreading that stuff around?

JACKIE
Come on, man, you're impossible; I'm not bothering you.

KATZ

You are. Bothering me. Go over there; get this stuff—

JACKIE

All right, come on. (*Gathering it up.*) I don't need a hassle. (*Moving.*) Man, I can't get my blood sugar up today. (*Sitting in lounge. Dumping her papers on the table: change-of-address cards, a copy of* Organic Gardening, *etc.*) I got about a dozen things to do here. I walked all over town this morning. We're getting out of here tomorrow.

JAMIE

Yeah?

JACKIE

I go to that insurance place; they give me a receipt for my money; I get that paper in my hand and we're gone.
(MRS. BELLOTTI *comes down the stairs, carrying a box, and exits.*)

GIRL

(*Almost a whisper. To* PAUL)
She's taking out her son's clothes. She's got a husband with his leg off, and her son's been kicked out of here, and the father has sugar diabetes and hates the son anyway. God. I hear something like that and I just want to lock myself in the bathroom, order a sausage and anchovy pizza, and eat the entire thing. (*Pause.*) I occupied the bathtub on my floor once for three straight hours. You know those assorted boxes of bath salts with eight different scents? I put in one of each. I called the Pizza Shack—they'll deliver any time of the day or night anywhere in the city. I have their number on my wall about that big, like it was one of those numbers you call in case of emergency. I ordered a pizza. I filled up the tub and sat there for three solid hours. There wasn't a single bubble in the tub by the time I got out. It took me

the rest of the day to unpucker. Of course . . . (*Raising her voice, using* JACKIE's *magazine for a megaphone.*) . . . Now, that's out. There's no more hot water. They're trying to get rid of us.

JACKIE

Come on, don't mess with that. I mean, you can look at it but don't mislay it.

GIRL

What is it?

JACKIE

(*Continuing to fill out cards; tossing it off.*)

That magazine you can't get on a newsstand. You have to order that magazine to come to your home. I gotta look up their offices 'cause I have to send them one of these change-of-address cards. You subscribe to it. You get one a month. It's fantastic. (*Pausing in her work a second.*) You know anything about growing rice?

GIRL

What?

JACKIE

Growing *rice?* It's a water plant, isn't it?

GIRL

I don't know.

JACKIE

'Cause rice is nature's most perfect food. Because of the balance of its nutrients. That's what this country ought to be growin' instead of all that fuckin' wheat. You know those plants out past Fort McHenry? You know what they do?

GIRL

They're sugar plants, I thought.

JACKIE

Refining. Sugar refining. They take natural sugar and turn it into shit. And then they pollute the atmosphere doing it. You can't get people to care about the environment. Of their own planet. Did you see *Planet of the Apes?*

GIRL

No. I wanted to.

JACKIE

Well, they knew what was happening. (*Back to the magazine.*) You ought to read that. You know the great discoveries? Like the discovery of bacteria; and the discovery of uranium; the discovery of sulphur drugs? Like that?

GIRL

(*Serious, nodding.*)

The discovery of penicillin . . .

JACKIE

Right. Well, the next major discovery—scientists are going to find this out, they're gonna be researching this. These people in this magazine already know it. (*Pause.*) Garlic.

MILLIE

What?

JACKIE

Garlic. It's biodegradable.

(MILLIE *and* PAUL *watch without expression; the* GIRL *listens seriously;* JAMIE *is aghast but excited.*)

You know DDT is out; DDT is killing us. You know that. (*Pause.*) Garlic juice. Has in it . . . (*Reaching for the magazine.*) . . . this is just one aspect; it has about four separate aspects . . . (*Finding it.*) . . . it has in it three separate "All-i-um Sul-phates." Three separate killers. Bug

85

killers. Which just happen to be the three separate strong-est bug killers known to man.

(JAMIE *says with her, "known to man."*)

There's three different articles about garlic in this one is-sue.

GIRL

Is it all right to eat it? Because I've eaten it.

JACKIE

Sure, it's good for you. That's the amazing thing. But—for the insecticide, what you do is: you take—this is what we're going to do. We may be the first. On this scale. You take detergent suds, and the juice from Mexican hot pep-pers, and garlic juice. And you mix those together and it'll kill anything.

MILLIE

I'd think it would.

JACKIE

But it won't hurt the worms. The earthworms. That's what you want, because they're necessary to you.

GIRL

What are they for?

JAMIE

(*As* JACKIE *starts to speak*)

Air.

JACKIE

A—a bunch of things. Different things. Where's your candy? (JAMIE *looks at* MR. KATZ.)

And . . . well, look at this. You probably never saw any-thing like this before. For real. (*She takes a paper from her purse—quite proud.*) That's a deed. A land deed. (*Hands it to the* GIRL.) That's for twenty acres. That's where our money went; that's a pretty good investment, considering. That's fifteen dollars an acre. We heard it advertised on the radio.

GIRL
That's fantastic. Where?
(*She hands it to* PAUL.)

JACKIE
(*Looking over* PAUL'*s shoulder.*)
It's all in here—we have to find it— "Two miles—" It goes for miles—that's how big it is—"south of Pepin and six miles west of—"

GIRL
Carter. Sure. Utah.

JACKIE
We were driving down from Buffalo, we heard—

GIRL
Are you from Buffalo? I didn't know that.

JACKIE
We was headed down to Florida to work on the crops; we heard this offer— I said to hell with pickin' somebody else's tomatoes; we'll raise our own crops.

GIRL
(*Unsure.*)
Sure . . .

JACKIE
We don't need no house. We're sleeping in a sleeping bag. If it rains, it gets nasty, we sleep in the car. We get sick of that, we move into a motel.

GIRL

How do you know there's a motel? If you've never been there?

JACKIE

Of course there's a motel; the country's gone to shit; there's always a motel.

GIRL

Don't you hate it? I spent the entire morning in a motel listening to some wheeler-dealer buying and selling most of the lumber south of the Mason Dix— (*Suddenly.*) Wait! Wait! Millie! Could I buy a railroad? Could I buy stock in a railroad? If I gave you six hundred dollars, could you go wherever it is and buy stock for me? Or could you take me there? And introduce me to your broker? Do you have a stockbroker?

MILLIE

No—I never had any interest in it; I only invested because there wasn't anything particular that I wanted. I wasn't interested in the stock—

GIRL

—You could go to the annual meetings; you could speak out—

MILLIE

—Oh, I don't know anything about it.

GIRL

You could tell them to shape up. Will you introduce me?

MILLIE

Surely; one day, if you're interested . . .

GIRL

Not one day. Not today because it's a holiday, but tomorrow.

MILLIE

Well, if you're still interested in it and you—

GIRL

—Come on, say yes.

MILLIE

If I feel like it, if you remind me.

GIRL

You don't live on this planet, Millie, you really don't.

MILLIE

No, I know, I never seemed to connect with the things—

GIRL

—I mean you're so sweet; a person just forgets completely how batty you are.

MILLIE

Fairly batty, I believe.

GIRL

Really, completely crackers sometimes.

MILLIE

—Well, not so bad as that, maybe—

GIRL

—But intelligent and all, you know—

MILLIE

—Oh, I was never completely stupid; just outside, I'm afraid, with no particular interest in peering in. When I realized that so much of people's preoccupation was in worldly houses, I realized that—

GIRL

I like that—worldly houses.

89

MILLIE

—that I was quite outside. I was one of fourteen, you know. I was the youngest of—

GIRL

Fourteen brothers and sisters?

MILLIE

Oh, I come from an enormous family; it wasn't at all unusual at the time; a huge old Victorian house outside Baton Rouge; an amazing old house, really, with—when you ask about spirits—oh, well, you couldn't keep track of them all. Banging doors, throwing silverware, breaking windows. They were all over the house. There was a black maid— slave girl, I suppose, and a revolutionary soldier and his girl, and a Yankee carpetbagger, and a saucy little imp of a girl who sashayed about very mischievously. She'd been pushed out of a window and was furious about it. Storming through the upstairs, slamming windows shut all over the house. It was quite an active place.

GIRL

Oh, I love it.

MILLIE

And when my aunt died—a wonderful old lady. It had been her husband's house. I must have been only eight or nine. She died and her sisters and brothers—my father even—scrabbled over her silverware and clothes and jewelry. Even the pots and pans. One cook ran off with all the cooking vessels. None of the things meant anything to my aunt, of course; she hardly realized she had them. I remember my father, with a Georgian silver teapot in one hand and an epergne in the other, yelling, "If Ariadne were alive she'd be scandalized!" And I thought, no, she wouldn't, Daddy, she'd be very amused. At all of you.

GIRL

And you're like her.

MILLIE

Not really. I'm very silly; she was quite a marvelous lady. You couldn't be like that today.

GIRL

I think you are. You had a cook? Who ran away with the—

MILLIE

Oh, yes, for some reason she decided to take every kerosene lamp and taper in the house. My uncle had been very frugal about them, so I suppose she thought they were valuable. She ordered a wagon and loaded it full. She was so foolish, that poor woman. Completely mad, of course. A wonderful old battle-ax. Carrying off vast old zinc tubs—four feet across. God knows what use they had, and big old copper vats and pans, skillets, spoons, wooden spoons, even the slop jars. While everyone was upstairs squabbling over the linen. They came down for supper—we had an enormous old-fashioned wood stove in the kitchen; she had managed to dismantle half of that before she gave up. (*Chuckles.*) I still remember all of them sitting around in the dark eating bread and jelly sandwiches. There wasn't even a coffeepot!

PAUL

I don't get it.

MILLIE

(*Hand on his knee, embrace.*)

Nor did I, Paul, I didn't get it at all. But I thought it was very amusing. (*Beat.*) Spirits are very peaceful, of course. They don't act up unless there's tension in a household. But oh, my! That night! Did they carry on! You've never heard such caterwauling!

GIRL

Oh! I want to see it! Spirits doing that! Don't you hope it's true? I mean scientifically true? I want them to come up with absolute scientific proof that there are spirits and ghosts and reincarnation. I want everyone to see them and talk to them. Something like that! Some miracle. Something huge! I want some *major miracle* in my lifetime!

JACKIE

Did you know the first two hours after you pick them, green beans lose twenty percent of their vitamin C?

GIRL

How much have they got?

JACKIE

A lot, but you shouldn't eat them. What you should eat is kale.

JAMIE

Kale.

JACKIE

It's a kind of lettuce. And lettuce has opium in it—if you know how to get it out.

JAMIE

(*With her*)

. . . to get it out.

MRS. OXENHAM

(*As* MRS. BELLOTTI *comes in and goes upstairs*)

Here's your party. Young man?

PAUL

(*Jumping up—going to the desk.*)

Me?

MRS. OXENHAM

This isn't going to tell you anything. It's just a rent receipt.

PAUL

Is that your signature?

MRS. OXENHAM

I can't remember every person who pays rent here two years later.

PAUL

He was very quiet and neat. He wore a derby. He had a very soft voice and he was—shit, don't you ever look at people?

MRS. OXENHAM

That's all I can tell you, I told you it wouldn't do any good.

PAUL

Do you remember if he left a forwarding address?

MRS. OXENHAM

We don't accept forwarding addresses.

PAUL

Grayish hair and—

MRS. OXENHAM

That's all I know; I don't remember him.

PAUL

Would you remember it if he fell dead in the lobby? If he was found in his room—?

MRS. OXENHAM

That didn't happen.
(*Phone.*)
Front desk. (*Writes down a number, looks in the book, and dials.*)

93

GIRL

He wore a derby?

PAUL

He was a workman. When he retired he wore a suit and a derby, because he wanted to look like he was retired . . .

GIRL

What is a derby? Really? (*Pause.*) Are you from a poor family?

PAUL

No.

GIRL

Oh. Were you close? To him?
(*Pause.*)

PAUL

He squinted a little . . .

GIRL

You were, weren't you? Close.

PAUL

He wanted to come live with Mom and Dad, and they wrote him they didn't have room for him. They didn't want him.
(*To* MILLIE)
He sang songs . . . all the time . . . under his breath . . . My sister . . .

GIRL

What? Your sister?

PAUL

She talked about him all the time . . . she told me about . . . what he was . . . like—like what he was like.

GIRL

She told you? Didn't you—ever meet him?

PAUL

How could I meet him, I was always off in some god-damned school.

GIRL

And you want—

PAUL

I want him! *I* have room for him!

GIRL

Well, don't take it out on me.

JACKIE

Where did he work?

PAUL

I called them. They started getting his pension checks back —they don't know where he is . . .

JACKIE

You finished with that, I don't want to lose that.
(*Magazine*—GIRL *hands it to her.*)

GIRL

What did he do?

PAUL

He worked. Mother's family had about a billion dollars' worth of whiskey distilleries—that's why Dad married— Granddad kept right on working. They were all so damn high-society they wouldn't associate with anyone like—

GIRL

You don't talk to the person you're talking to. Did anybody ever tell you that? You talk to yourself. You don't look at people.

PAUL
(*Glowers at her. Finally*)
He was an engineer.

GIRL
Oh, God; every boy in Phoenix Central High was "going into engineering"; that's all they ever talked about was their T squares and slide rules. I never did tell them I didn't know what engineering was; maybe you can tell me. What'd he do? Exactly?

PAUL
(*Glowers.*)
He was—

GIRL
—Relax.

PAUL
Huh?

GIRL
Relax. You're all tense. You're just like a— You're all tense. (*Pause.*) What'd he do?
(*Pause.*)

PAUL
Who?

GIRL
Your granddad?

PAUL
He was an engineer. For the railroad. He drove the Baltimore and Ohio between—

GIRL
(*On "Ohio," standing, bursting into tears.*)
NO! No! Oh! Oh! He drove a train! Oh, I want to meet him! I want to talk to him!

PAUL

Well, you find him; you think of a way and I'll let you talk to him.

GIRL

Somewhere! You don't know. How I feel! You can, too. If he was here, of course you can find him. Stay for Bill; I'll help you. Oxenham isn't any good, she wouldn't look for her own grandfather—and I don't even know the day people; the afternoon people are temporary and, anyway, I got to get some sleep and Bill comes on at twelve.

PAUL

I was here last night.

GIRL

Yes, but you didn't tell us what you were doing—dummy—why didn't you say something?

PAUL

I gotta be somewhere tomorrow.

GIRL

Come on, everyone's gotta be somewhere tomorrow; I want to meet him. Where was his run? Do you know? Did you know him at all?

JACKIE

Come on, don't jiggle the table.

MILLIE

I think—

(MR. MORSE *has been coming down the stairs— He works his mouth, waves his arms, but no words come out.* MILLIE *stands.* KATZ *goes to him.* MRS. OXENHAM *stands. The* GIRL *sees him.* JACKIE *does too. Finally, almost reaching the landing.*)

MORSE

Been-been-taken-everything-that-person. I been robbed. I been robbed.

KATZ

What?

(JACKIE *starts to leave.*)

MORSE

That person.

KATZ

Where you going? You were up there, weren't you?

JACKIE

I got things to attend to.

KATZ

You're not attending to no more business for a minute.

JAMIE

She didn't touch your things. She hasn't been near your things.

KATZ

You just keep out of it.

JACKIE

I helped him out with a problem he had. I don't know what you're talking about. You been picking on me ever since I came here. That's all you know, because you don't like the way I look or the way I dress or something! You don't like the way I live!

MORSE	KATZ
That's the person. Took my wife's things. That's all I have in this world.	All I'm saying is, give it back. Turn it over to him. And all of it and this minute. Everything you took.

JAMIE
She didn't go up there.

What's missing, Mr. Morse? What are you missing from your room?

MORSE
What?

KATZ
What's gone, what are you missing?

MORSE
My things! My wedding cuff links and my necklace that belonged to my wife! And my mother!

JACKIE
Yeah, well, I didn't take his fucking mother; he's crazy.

MORSE
And four rings; a gold ring and a sapphire ring and—I don't remember . . .

JACKIE
(*Overlapping from "sapphire"*)
I got things to do—you can search my car and you can search my room— I've got nothing to hide; we got business.

KATZ
(*Grabbing her.*)
You're not leaving.

JACKIE
Why me? Why not somebody else? Let me go or I'll kill you, you son of a bitch—

KATZ
(*Struggling with her.*)
Give me her purse—
(GIRL *shakes her head.*)

Give me her damn— (*Wrenching it away from her; dumping it on the floor.*) I been listening to you talking about pawnshops.

JACKIE
(*Flailing; but held back by one arm.*)
No; get out of my personal things. That belongs to me—those things belong to me.
(*As* KATZ *finds a knotted silk man's sock at the bottom of her purse*)
That ain't his. Stop it!

MORSE
Give me that! Give me my things!!
(KATZ *hands it to him.*)

KATZ
That right there could get you ten years!

JACKIE
I got dreams, goddamnit! What's he got?
(KATZ *lets go of her.* MORSE *goes to the stairs.*)
(*She sags into a chair.*)
What's he got?

MORSE
(*Deeply shaken.*)
I'm going to report this incident.

KATZ
You're going up to your room. You got your stuff—is that all of it?

JACKIE
(*Weakly*)
You robbed me.

MORSE
I'm calling the police.

JAMIE
I'll beat you up!

KATZ
Your phone's out of order. It's your own damn fault to let people in your room.

MORSE
(*Going up and off; mumbling.*)
I have my rights.

KATZ
You got no rights here.
(*To* JACKIE)
I want you and your brother both out of here tonight.

JACKIE
I'm paid up here till—

KATZ
I'll refund your rent money—out tonight, or I turn you in myself.

GIRL
Not from Mr. Morse. He doesn't have anything. He never hurt anybody.

JACKIE
You ripped off one of your scores, you told me so.

GIRL
He could afford it.

JACKIE
Just because you have protection. (*Returning pen.*) I don't

want you thinking I'm taking your fuckin' ink pen. (*At desk.*)

GIRL
I wasn't going to tell you, but you got nothing.

JACKIE
I got what I need.

GIRL
That land you got won't grow nothing. I know that place. I may not know much but I know that—

JACKIE
What are you talking about? You're a liar—you don't know anything about it. That's farmland.

GIRL
—because I been there. On the Rio Grande Zephyr. It's nothing but a desert—a salt desert, it don't even grow cactus. Six miles west of Carter, two miles south of Pepin —it's desert for a hundred miles.

JACKIE
It's farmland! That's farmland! I got brochures. I got pictures.

GIRL
Even I know better than to buy land from the radio. You can't get farmland for that price nowhere. You ought to be ashamed of yourself, robbing Mr. Morse.

JACKIE
(*Snatching up the deed, putting it in her purse.*)
I know what I'm doing for my brother and . . .
(*Goes about collecting her things— She knows instinctively that it is true.*) You may not know anything about grow-

ing . . . we know what we're doing. (*She blindly collects her papers, stuffing them into her bag.*)
(*Pause.*)

JAMIE
That's not fair . . .

JACKIE
Be still.

GIRL
Or maybe . . . maybe I'm wrong. Maybe I have it mixed up. I don't want to hurt anybody.

JACKIE
Ain't nobody been hurt by you or . . .

JAMIE
Anybody. (*He is about to burst into tears.*) You're—

JACKIE
(*Crying out.*)
Shut up! (*Looks around, sits, falls into a chair.*) Boy . . . everything I try . . . (*Pause.*) I liked you, too. Well. We live and learn. (*Getting up, taking her purse and bag.*)

GIRL
Oh, Jesus.

JACKIE
Come on. We're gonna go eat.
(JAMIE *goes out.*)
We were getting out of here tomorrow, a few hours one way or the— (*The energy drains from her; her mind scattered, she stands blindly holding back tears.*)

GIRL
Jackie?
(JACKIE *starts and runs out, the* GIRL *runs after her.*)

Maybe it was a lie. I was just mad. I haven't had any sleep.
Forget I said it. Please.

(MRS. BELLOTTI *immediately comes down the stairs and follows them out, carrying another box.* MILLIE *has moved to
the shadows of the stairway.* PAUL *stands in the center of
the lobby.*)

MILLIE

Your grandfather is alive, Paul.

(*The lights begin to fade. He looks for her, sees her.*)

PAUL

Where is he?

MILLIE

Oh, I have no idea. I don't know him. I never met him. I
only know that he isn't dead.

PAUL

How do you know?

MILLIE

I don't know how I know. I never know how I know; I just
know he isn't dead.

(MILLIE *and* PAUL *freeze. The lights are very dim.* KATZ *and*
MRS. OXENHAM *prepare and leave.* BILL *enters and turns on
the radio.* MILLIE *moves upstairs.* PAUL *stares after her as
the music from the radio spreads to the house and the lights
dim out.*)

Act Three

(*Midnight. On stage,* BILL *and* MR. MORSE. BILL *is at the switchboard.* MR. MORSE *sits in the lounge, not at ease.* BILL *opens a sack from a deli and takes out a sweet roll. He takes a sip of coffee from a paper container. He glances at a note left on the board, plugs in the board while still standing, glancing at the clock. Rings. Sips coffee.*)

BILL

It's twelve- (*Glance at clock.*) oh-six. You getting up? Good morning—Billy Jean, Lilac Lavender, Martha. No, no talk, come down if you want to gab.
(*As* APRIL *appears, descending the stairs, wearing a long diaphanous gown*)
April's down here.

APRIL
(*To herself*)
Down, down, down . . .

BILL

No, I got work to do.
(*Disconnects, smiling at the phone. Then to* APRIL)
Look at you, done up fit to kill.

APRIL

That seems to be the consensus. Evening, Mr. Morse, baby.

BILL

One of those nights, huh?

APRIL

Bill, tonight wasn't even in the book. You see that john just walked out of here?

BILL

Didn't pay any attention to him.

APRIL

Just the least bit flaky.

BILL

Yeah? What's the problem?

APRIL

If my clientele represents a cross section of American manhood, the country's in trouble.

BILL

I'd think it would be.

APRIL

I don't need it from you this morning. I called Martha's pizza palace and ordered a pizza, that's how bad it is.

BILL

That bad, huh? You get to bed?

APRIL

(*She laughs.*)

No, Bill, what can I tell you? It was one of those nights. The room got a workout. I turned fifteen on the floor, twenty in the tub, and fifteen across the top of the dresser. I'm not lying. Definitely flaky. Usually I can count on one in five getting a little experimental.

BILL
Not today, huh?

APRIL
Today we drew a full house. (*Laughs.*) Guy says, "What's that?" I say, "That's the tub, that's where I keep the alligator, better stay back: you ain't got nothing you can afford to lose." Says, "I'd kinda like to make it in the tub." I say, "Honey, look: you ever see one of these? It's a bed. It's kinda kinky but let me show you how it works." End up, we make it in—

BILL
(*Said with her*)
In the tub.

APRIL
Right. Tell him all we got is cold water, it's gonna do you no good; nothing would do. (*Laughs.*) He gets in, sits down, I turn on the water and nearly scalded his balls off.

BILL
I got it fixed.

APRIL
Yeaaah! Spanking red from the butt down. Loved it. Stayed in for twenty minutes. Very groovy experience for him. If I knew he was coming, I'd have dug out the rubber duck.

BILL
Anything to get somebody to like you.

APRIL

Like me? Pay me. They know me from the wallpaper.
(*To* MR. MORSE)
Don't they, darlin'?

MR. MORSE

It's too hot.

APRIL

You noticed that, did you?

MR. MORSE

It's no good for my health. You got to have circulation of air. This hotel is overheated. They're trying to make us all sick.

APRIL

See that. There's always a logical explanation for everything.

GIRL

(*Entering in a terry robe and slippers.*)
Morning, Bill. Morning, honey.

BILL

You get any sleep?

GIRL

Did I? I fainted. Besides, with Oxenham guarding the gates, there wasn't any point. She is absolutely no help at all. Where's Paul? That guy?

BILL

No messages.

GIRL

You seen him since you been on? That guy who feel asleep in the lobby last night.

BILL
Went out; left his bag.

GIRL
(*Shaking herself awake.*)
Oh, golly! Brufff! Oh, it's getting warm. Cross your fingers. Maybe it's finally spring.

BILL
Supposed to get up to seventy today.

APRIL
Two more weeks and everything will stink.

GIRL
(*Taking a bit of his roll.*)
Anyway, we got a project.

BILL
You do, huh? Come on, that's breakfast.

GIRL
Not *me*. *We* do. (*She goes to the files.*)

BILL
Don't pull that crap—what are you doing?

GIRL
Didn't your mother ever tell you; the first warm day you start the cleaning. (*Occupied with pulling out boxes of files.*)

BILL
(*Over*)
No joke, that stuff's dirty. Wear some clothes when you come down here.

GIRL
Come on, I told Paul you'd help him or he would have given up, so you got to help too.

BILL

Oxenham will have your hide; you know that.

GIRL

I'll put them back. I figure there are all those boxes in the basement. I can go through those too.

BILL

What boxes?

GIRL

Don't you even explore your own place of business?

BILL

(*Buzzer rings.*)

I just work here. There's rats down there; you can't go down—come on.

(*As she dumps a pile of boxes*)

What are you doing? What do you want with those?

GIRL

Answer your phone.

BILL

(*Into the phone.*)

Hold it.

GIRL

That fellow who was here—

APRIL

Freak.

GIRL

That freak who was here is looking for his "long-lost grand-dad." Everyone has been about as helpful as a stick. And we're going to find some trace of the old man. Something to go on.

BILL
(*Phone.*)
Yeah? (*Dials.*) Don't pull those things out here.

GIRL
Don't you like mysteries? Don't you want to help someone? Besides, you're going to anyway, because I volunteered you. The man may be lost; he may have amnesia; he was a train-man, Bill. He drove the B and O for twenty-six years. And he's in there.

BILL
(*Phone.*)
They don't answer. (*Disconnects.*) I don't know where the hell you get your energy. How long did you sleep?

GIRL
Long. Six hours or more. April, where were you for the action? You missed the excitement.

APRIL
I saw plenty of action: you're right, I missed the excitement.

GIRL
Did you hear about the— Did you tell them, Mr. Morse?

APRIL
Mr. M. is none too spry tonight.

GIRL
Where are they? Jackie and Jamie? Did they leave?

BILL
Who's that?

APRIL
Flotsam and Jetsam?

BILL

Note here says three-nineteen's checking out. Car's not out front.

APRIL

Don't tell me that heap actually moves.

GIRL

It better move, they've been eighty-sixed.

BILL
(*Mock disappointment.*)
Awww, that's too bad.

GIRL

I gotta have something. You want a cup of tea?

BILL

I could stand a cup of tea. There any water in there?

GIRL

Yeah, it's fine. April?

APRIL

Huh? Yeah, sure. What?

GIRL

Tea. Mr. Morse?

APRIL

Like a cup of tea, Mr. Morse?

MORSE

Too hot.

GIRL

This will take forever.

JAMIE
(*Entering.*)
Has Jackie been here?

BILL
Don't know; I just got on.
(*Sotto voce to* APRIL)
Is he Flotsam or is he—

APRIL
He's a sweetie, aren't you, baby? We thought you were gone. Is who here?

JAMIE
Is Jackie back yet?

APRIL
Ain't seen—her. Where's she supposed to be?

JAMIE
(*Looking at the* GIRL.)
She went to get gas for the car.

GIRL
Morning, Jamie. Are you speaking to me?
(*Beat.*)

JAMIE
Morning.

GIRL
You look sleepy; you sleepy?
(*He is—shakes his head no.*)
What time did you get up?

JAMIE
Six.

APRIL
You had a nap?

GIRL
Six this morning?

JAMIE
Every morning.

APRIL
You helping her carry things down?

JAMIE
She took her stuff—I have to take my own, though. That's the way we do it.

GIRL
(*Back to files.*)
This is going to be a snap.

APRIL
What time did she go out for gas?
(*Beat.*)

JAMIE
'Bout six.

APRIL
This evening. Well, see, she's probably looking for natural gas.

JAMIE
No lead.

APRIL
(*To* BILL)
No way.
(*Phone buzzes.*)

BILL
Four-three-oh-seven.

APRIL
(*To* JAMIE)

116

Honey, I don't really think it's necessary to drag down a lot of things till she gets here.

JAMIE
(*He looks to the front door and hardly takes his eyes off it.*)
This is it.

BILL
(*Holding receiver.*)
Billy Jean? Billy Jean?

GIRL
"Billy Jean"? That's three weeks ago. I can't, I'm in the middle—ask who it is—he won't tell you.

APRIL
Here! (*Rushes to the phone.*) Hello, this is Miss Billy Jean's "girl"; she's in the tub; could I ask who's calling her, please? (*Pause.*) Umm hmmm. I'll tell her. It's Mr. Last-month-all-night-at-the-Statler-Hilton, madam, shall I toss him in?

GIRL
Oh, God. What do you call it when a guy has really terrible breath?

APRIL
Par for the run.

GIRL
Well, this guy has a terminal case of par for the run.
(*Gives herself completely to phone.*)
Hi. You're back. Of course I do, silly, Penthouse B.

APRIL
(*Poking* BILL.)
Penthouse B.

GIRL

It's great to *talk* to you; only I'm freezing. I will not, you could get electrocuted.

BILL
For what?

APRIL
Talking on the phone in the tub.

GIRL

Well, that's a lot better, only I can't. Mom's in town; isn't it a drag? You did? Was that all you liked? That wasn't my fault if I got a little carried away. Listen, could I send over a great friend?
(APRIL *laughs.*)
O.K., then just call Veda. But you call me back when you're in town again, you hear? I won't promise anything; not with you. Bye, bye. (*Hangs up.*) Jesus. Can you imagine the drag? Dinner and eight hours in the feathers and he thinks he's Rockefella giving you fifty dollars.

BILL
I don't like you taking those calls down here.

GIRL

You gave it to me. (*Back to books.*) I mean, if a person is interested in making any money, the man ought to realize. The money's in turnover, not in lay there.

SUZY
(*Comes clicking down the stairs, carrying four small suit-cases, setting them down. She is dressed in a skin-tight, very short pink suit.*)
That's just the first load. Don't anybody get up. I got it arranged so I can do it all myself.

118

BILL

That's a pretty snappy outfit, Suzy.

SUZY

(*Going.*)

Don't you just love it?

(*Gone.*)

APRIL

I kinda liked that pink jobby she had on last night. Would you look at that luggage? That girl has got to be the cheapest whore in town.

GIRL

I got it! I got one. See? (*Pokes* BILL.) I'll bet I haven't been here five minutes. Oxenham could have told him that; he didn't ask any leading questions.

BILL

What have you got?

GIRL

I know when he left. I got them renting his room out.

(*To other files.*)

Now what? I don't know what half of this stuff is. Letters. Terrific—

BILL

Come on.

GIRL

What if he wrote to change his address or send things? Or any of a thousand reasons. That's where you'd find a return address—

BILL

(*Overlap*)

Put those rent books back in there—

GIRL

—When I'm finished. Why don't you let me cover the board and you go out and get us a hamburger before they close.

BILL

April ordered a pizza.

APRIL

Yeah, ought to be here any minute.

GIRL

Thank God; you're a sister of mercy. What's this? Wrong year. See, I know when he left. I only have to look at the one month or a little after. What's in the broom closet; there's dozens of boxes in there; they're probably years old, aren't they?

BILL

I haven't been in there.

JAMIE

Excuse me . . .

GIRL

(*Looks up—slows down some.*)
Me? What, Jamie . . . ?

JAMIE

I don't know your name . . .

GIRL

I know—I'm working on it. What's wrong, honey?

JAMIE

Did you really go there? (*Pause.*) We heard that the Mormons was good farmers . . .

GIRL

I imagine they are. They've irrigated all the— Jamie, there

aren't any Mormons *near* where your land is; there's nothing near there. I mean, I didn't get out, but it's just white sand—it's salt and soda, it looks like. Cactus can't even grow there.

JAMIE
If we brought water, we could . . .

GIRL
Jamie, you irrigate that land, you'd have twenty acres of Bromo-Seltzer.

SUZY
(*With two more pieces of unmatched luggage and a box tied with an extension cord.*)
Listen, I'll be right back down. I got a surprise.

BILL
What's happening? Are you checking out?

SUZY
(*Dumps it.*)
Yes, love; do up my bill. Take it out of—here—take it out of that. Don't anybody leave the lobby; you gotta promise me. (*She is gone.*)

APRIL
You gotta give it to her; the girl really knows what looks good on her.

GIRL
God, this is going to be depressing.

APRIL
What's that?

GIRL
No, I won't read them. God, they're depressing. All filed away. Nobody will ever answer them.

BILL

Just look at the envelope; you don't have to read them.

GIRL

I know, but I can't help it. Half of this is from the Welfare Department—from everywhere. I sat down over in the park and this perfectly normal-looking woman sat down. Well dressed, sixty years old—and she started talking to me . . . Jesus. It really gets me that a normal person never opens her mouth. It's only the crazies that'll talk to you.

APRIL

What's her story?

GIRL

Oh . . . she feeds dogs. Stray dogs. She goes around to all the butcher shops, and for three hours every day she feeds the poor stray dogs—I mean, it's probably a good thing to do; but you got to be crazy even to do anything good. She says isn't it wonderful to be able to have something like that. Says she considers herself lucky because there's so many dogs in Baltimore.

APRIL

I consider myself *un*lucky because there's so many dogs in Baltimore.

GIRL

I think she was trying to convert me.

BILL

Come on, you're getting filthy there. Look at that.

APRIL

I always say if a lady—

GIRL

(*As* PAUL *enters*)
Where have you been? Where'd you go?

PAUL

I went to eat.

GIRL

Did you bring anything back, I'm starving. April, where's that pizza? Never mind— Look; come here and look; my God, I'm not going to do this by myself.

PAUL

(*To the desk.*)
What is it?

GIRL

Just follow this. Room two-oh-three—that's your granddad's receipt. That's for December 14—that's probably the one Oxenham showed you—they go back forever—but—look at this. December 21 I didn't find anything—nothing for his room at all. Then. December 28. J. Smith. Room two-oh-three. So he left between the fourteenth and the twenty-first of December. Probably on the twenty-first, when his week was up.

PAUL

Doesn't really matter . . .

GIRL

It's a fact. A first fact. If we're going to call like the Salvation Army or flophouses or hospitals, we've got a specific date. You can't expect them to look through six months of records. Also, I have a cop friend on the pussy posse, but I don't think I should go to them first thing—on account of your experience. We don't want them getting curious.

PAUL

That doesn't tell you anything.

GIRL

It certainly does! You came here knowing nothing; you've got to narrow it down.

(*The sound of a train.*)
Listen! Son of a bitch. What time is it?

BILL
(*Glances at clock.*)
Twelve—[whatever]

GIRL
An hour and a half late. Jesus. And that's good. And they're conscientious. The engineers—it's not their fault; it's everyone else doesn't give a— Still, it's better than yesterday, they sailed through at five-thirty; they might as well just cancel the whole run; tell people to take the planes. I really have no use for airplanes; I'd be just as happy if every one fell into the sea like what's his name.

PAUL
Icarus.

GIRL
No, it was Gary Cooper or Cary Grant; I get them all mixed up. The Continental came through this afternoon on time —I sent the front office a telegram of congratulations—I honestly did. Anyway, besides this, phone calls: they keep a record of every outgoing call; we could find people in town he called. He must have known someone. Nobody's so shy they don't know someone. I don't care what kind of hat he wore.

SUZY
(*Flushed, coming down the stairs with two bottles of champagne and a shopping bag.*)
All right, here it is. This is it; it's cold too; I've had it in the fridge all afternoon. Bill, open this up, we're having a toast. I called the cab already, kids, so we just got a minute, but that ain't cheating us out of a little party.

APRIL
Open it, Bill.

JAMIE
Are you going too?

SUZY
I sure am, honey. I don't need to have a place falling down around me before I take action. I got paper cups and everything. Mr. Morse, you're going to have a drink, honey, aren't you? It's nice and cold.

APRIL
He'll love it.

BILL
It's morning for me; I'm not on your schedule.

SUZY
That's the best time in the world to drink it; champagne doesn't have a time to drink it. Come on. I just wish we had some nuts. I didn't have time to think of everything.

JAMIE
I got some. In my bag.

SUZY
That's all right, honey, they're yours, we don't—
(*She is pouring.*)

JAMIE
No, I got lots of them. (*He takes two large jars from his bag.*)

SUZY
Don't anybody drink till we have a toast.

APRIL
Where the hell did you get those?

JAMIE

We always have them; we got a whole case of them.

APRIL

Jesus Christ, they're soy beans.

JAMIE

They're great for you. And they're good.

GIRL

I want something, if I'm going to be drinking champagne; I've not had a bite.

SUZY

Hold your cup, honey. This is the real stuff.
(*Next is* PAUL.)
Take a cup.

PAUL

No, thanks, I'm not—
(*To* BILL)
I got a bag in—

SUZY

(*Overlapping*)
Yes, come on; we may be a flophouse, but we know class: see, I remember. Only nobody else, 'cause there ain't that much; if anybody comes in, we're just drinking ginger ale.

BILL

(*Raising his glass.*)
Uh . . . uh . . . To Suzy!

SUZY

(*Immensely pleased.*)
No! Not to me! Come on, to this place! To . . .

APRIL

To us!

ALL
To us!
(*They drink the toast and make appropriately enthusiastic responses.*)
This is the real stuff.

APRIL
These things are good.

GIRL
They are, they're great.

SUZY
You can't eat soy beans with champagne! Well, that's sweet, honey—isn't he cute—where's the dy—his sister?

APRIL
She went for "gas." At six o'clock. This afternoon. She'll be right back.

SUZY
Oh. (*Beat.*) Hey, these are real good. What'd you say they was?

JAMIE
Barbecue-flavor soy beans. With sea salt and tomato powder.

APRIL
I think it's the sea salt that does it.

SUZY
O.K. One more round. There's plenty more. While it lasts. (*Pouring around.*) This is California champagne. This isn't that New York State stuff. One of my johns told me the difference. New York wines are made with a whole different kind of grape. It's all in the grape.

GIRL

I didn't know champagne was made out of grapes. I thought—

APRIL

What'd you think it was made out of, soy beans?

SUZY

(*Overlapping a bit*)

Sure it is; California grapes are the same grapes they use in the French champagne. The Frenchies brought them over and planted them in California. In New York they got the wrong grape!

APRIL

Cheers, everybody.

SUZY

(*Overlapping*)

I love champagne because you got to share it with people; sittin' around drinking champagne all by yourself without an event would be like jerkin' off.

APRIL

Well, we got a first-class event here.

GIRL

I'll tell you one thing I'm not going to do; I'm not going to move from here.

APRIL

I'm with you. We'll throw ourselves in front of the wrecking ball.

GIRL

Besides, I have a friend who knows law and I hate to blow it on the one month's notice, but it's three months'. And then we don't have to move.

PAUL
(*To* BILL)
They all got friends into something.

GIRL
Baltimore used to be one of the most beautiful cities in America.

APRIL
Every city in America used to be one of the most beautiful cities in America.

GIRL
And this used to be a beautiful place. They got no business tearing it down. April and me and Mr. Morse and Millie. And Jamie.

SUZY
That's a delegation with balls.

GIRL
Where's Millie?

BILL
Millie went to bed. Said she was gonna try to sleep.

SUZY
She ought to be having some of this.

BILL
They might not get it torn down. They got a committee now to try to save it.

SUZY
Yeah, they also got antique people calling every ten minutes making bids on the door knobs. My money's on the vultures every time.

APRIL

This is fantastic stuff, Suzy. You're a dedicated woman.

GIRL

Who would we go to to make a protest?

SUZY

Only . . . (*With pride.*) . . . I got to tell you. I'm not moving into another hotel. I got an apartment. On the twelfth floor. It's got five rooms. There's a doorman; there's only one other girl sharing it with me.

APRIL

Wait; this is very familiar—

SUZY

—She's a sweetheart. She's read everything ever printed. Even newspapers.

APRIL

A wife-in-law.

SUZY

—Well, there's nothing in the arrangement that calls for that tone of voice. And I can have a pet if I want one. And I do. I've longed for a pet. I love animals.

APRIL

People who keep animals in the house are sick. Pets and pimps.

SUZY

I would be very good to an animal.

APRIL

I don't care, it's still sick.

SUZY

I have great love for animals.

GIRL
What kind of an animal?

SUZY
All kinds. All animals. Puppies and kittens and little calves and ponies, and all of them.

APRIL
And a cuddly little woolly black pimp.

SUZY
All non-human animals. And fish. I don't like tropical fish.

APRIL
My husband used to keep fish.

GIRL
I didn't know you were married.

APRIL
I didn't either.
(*To* SUZY)
Who is it?

BILL
What's a wife-in-law?

GIRL
(*Overlapping*)
Come on, Bill, how long have you worked here?

APRIL
(*Overlapping*)
Ask Suzy about wife-in-law arrangements. She's the authority—

SUZY
(*Overlapping*)
It's nothing like that. She *asked me;* I'll be the wife, honey.

131

I'm nobody's second fiddle. You don't have to worry about me. She's just there to keep house as far as we're concerned —she'll be the in-law. She can't turn two hundred a day.

APRIL
Who is he? Are you going back with Eddie?

SUZY
I certainly am not. Who do you think I am? I may have a soft spot in my heart but I don't want—

APRIL
(*Overlapping*)
You got a soft spot in your head.

SUZY
—This man is not like that. Eddie was a pimp; this man is a man.

APRIL
Who's the boy friend this time?

SUZY
Not this time. This is my first *real friend*. Eddie was a pimp.

APRIL
You're telling me; a pimp fink.

SUZY
This man is a man!

APRIL
Yeah, what does he do?

SUZY
He does nothing! And he does it *gorgeously!*

BILL
How'd you get talked into another arrangement like that?

APRIL

They don't talk, they croon.

SUZY

Tell me you don't need someone; maybe you don't, but I do;
I need love!

APRIL

All you have to say to a hooker is cottage small by the water-
fall and they fold up.

SUZY

You know I don't appreciate that word.

APRIL

Whadda you call it?

SUZY

I am not a that-word; I am a friendly person and it gets me
in trouble.

APRIL

—You're a professional trampoline.

SUZY

That is why I'm leaving! Derision! Derision! Because I'm
attacked with derision every time I try to do something
wonderful. Driven into the arms of a common pimp!
(APRIL *hoots.*)

GIRL

We're just thinking about you, Suzy.

APRIL

(*Overlapping*)
You've been down this road.

BILL

(*Overlapping*)
How's this one any better than Eddie?

SUZY

Just don't worry about it. Billy's never beat up one of his wives . . . ever!

APRIL

Jesus God, she's going with Billy Goldhole.

SUZY

That is not his name. And to call him by that name is to show your ignorance. And if you say he's beat up on anybody, I don't believe it.

CAB DRIVER	APRIL
(*Entering.*)	Go on, I don't want to have
Somebody here order a taxi?	anything to do with you.

SUZY

Yes. Here! This here. (*She starts to pick up some of the luggage.*)

CAB DRIVER

I'm not a moving van, lady. What is this?

SUZY

This stuff here; you can't take it quick enough.

CAB DRIVER	SUZY
I'm double-parked out	Don't sweat it, mister. I'm
there. I can't take all that.	taking my share. I'll pay
Where you going to? With	double the meter.
this crap?	

SUZY

I'm leaving this hole. Hole. Hole. Move it.

CAB DRIVER

I said I'm double-parked out there, lady. I'm not in the—

SUZY

You're double-parked. Tell me about it. The whole fuckin'

country is double-parked. I hope they tear down the place with all *(Picking up almost all the luggage as she rants.)* you in it. Goody-two-shoes included. I'm just sorry I gave you a little party. You don't know enough to appreciate it.

CAB DRIVER
Come on, lady, shake it.

SUZY
Shove it.
(They exit.)

GIRL
She's got to be the worst judge of character in Baltimore.

APRIL
She's gotta be the worst character in Baltimore.

BILL
She drew the cops here four times in one night once.

APRIL
Whadda you say, Mr. Morse? Unstable woman, huh?

MR. MORSE
(Who has not been following; still holds his untasted cup.)
Very good. Thank you.

GIRL
I wonder if the apartment has eleven-foot ceilings.

APRIL
It's got an eleven-inch licorice lollipop is what it's got.

SUZY
(Bursting back into the lobby, bawling. Super-emotional, hugs them in turn while speaking and is gone with the last word.)
I'm sorry. I know you love me. I can't leave like that. Mr.

Morse. We been like a family, haven't we? My family. Baby. I'm not that horrible. I can't be mad. Bill. I'll always remember this.
(*Gone.*)
(*A few seconds of stupefied, gawking silence.*)

PAUL
I got a bag back there.

BILL
Yeah. (*Handing it to him.*)

GIRL
Hey. Paul. You're supposed to be doing this with me. You're supposed to be helping.

PAUL
No, that's O.K. You don't have to do that.

GIRL
Did you find him? While you were out?

PAUL
(*Overlapping*)
Of course I didn't find him; he's gone. That doesn't tell you anything.

GIRL
Well, we knew he was gone; the thing we're trying to do is find him.

PAUL
He could be anywhere.

GIRL
He could be *some*where.

PAUL
It's not your problem. It was a bad idea. Thanks.

GIRL

You got room for him, I thought. Hey. *Talk,* for God's sake. You're worse than a dummy, at least they use sign language. What are you doing?

PAUL

I'm trying to go, do you mind?

GIRL

How can you be so interested in something—

PAUL

—Would you get off my back? What's your problem? I didn't ask for you to help me. I didn't ask you.

APRIL

She volunteered. You got some gripe, write to her; she collects stamps.

GIRL

Oh, I do not.

PAUL

Look, you're probably being very nice; but thanks, anyway, O.K.? Granddad isn't here. They don't know where he is. Nobody here knows where he is. It's all the same.

GIRL

Not yet; but I can find him. Nobody vanishes.

PAUL

It's just as well, probably. I got things to do.

GIRL

—It just isn't as easy as you thought. You been bitching Oxenham for being no help. Let us help.

PAUL

I wanted to find him. He'd move out of a place like this the

first chance he got; he wasn't a derelict. You don't know him.
(MILLIE *begins to come down the stairs.*)

GIRL
I said I wanted to know him.

APRIL
Hey, Millie.

MILLIE
(*Vaguely*)
Oh . . . hello, then . . .

PAUL
(*Mumbled*)
Well, I'm sorry . . .

BILL
Thought you were sleeping.
(*She raises a hand as if to say, That isn't important.*)

GIRL
Millie, tell him not to give up. Tell him we can find him
or he's gonna just give up.

MILLIE
Oh, that's too bad.

APRIL
Ought to be easy enough to find. Ten-foot white-haired
giant. Chops down cherry trees; doesn't lie about it.

GIRL
Come on, April; he was a trainman.

PAUL
Thanks, anyway, I'm sorry I got you involved. I'm not calling the Salvation— (*Begins to go.*)

GIRL

I *like* getting involved. Paul? You know what armor is? I had a scientologist tell me this. You're tied in knots all through your— Are you going to keep on looking for him? (*Silence*—PAUL *glares at her.*)

APRIL

Knock once for yes and—

PAUL

It's not your business one way or the other, is it? (*To them quietly*) Thanks very much, anyway. Thanks for your interest.

GIRL

(*Over "thanks very"*) You don't care about him. What if he's in— (*He goes.*) —some home for the— You! Boy, you're a—

APRIL

Creep.

GIRL

Creep. Well, I don't know if he doesn't really care or if we scared him off.

BILL

You can't help people who don't want it.

GIRL

I think he probably has trouble making friends.

APRIL

I think he has trouble making water. (*Pause. To* MILLIE) Have a drink of Suzy's champagne. Help you sleep.

MILLIE
(*Taking a cup.*)
Oh, I doubt that.

GIRL
Well, damn piss hell poot.

BILL
Just watch your language back here, O.K.?

APRIL
(*Pouring.*)
Come on . . .

GIRL
(*Dialing the phone.*)
No, it makes me . . .

APRIL
Bill?

BILL
Don't get me drunk here, now.

APRIL
Jamie? Come on. We won't tell her.
(JAMIE *comes to get the drink and goes back to the lounge.*)

GIRL
(*On the phone.*)
Penthouse B. Is he in the dining room? Well, tell him Billy Jean— No, don't bother; I couldn't bear it. No message. (*Hangs up.*) I could just kill Paul Granger. That's why nothing gets done; why everything falls down. Nobody's got the conviction to act on their passions.

APRIL
Go kill him then.

GIRL

I mean, it's his idea to find him. I don't think it matters what someone believes in. I just think it's really chicken not to believe in anything!

BILL
(*Pouring another.*)
Come on, join us.

GIRL

No, I'm going to take a bath while there's hot water. I'm just filthy.

BILL
Come on, drink to Suzy.

GIRL
(*Taking the cup—to* MILLIE)
Suzy left us.

MILLIE
Again?

APRIL
Exactly. God help her.

GIRL
(*Drinks.*)
I hate that. You like that, Jamie?

JAMIE
It's O.K.

MILLIE
Well. I've got no business down here.

APRIL
Drinking champagne, huh?

GIRL

I'm going up too.

(*She starts upstairs;* BILL *starts to pick up the books. Pre-occupied.*)

Don't you put those away; I'm not finished with those.

(BILL *looks off after her, aching.*)

APRIL

(*Snaps her fingers lightly at him. One. Two. Three. Four.*)

Hey. Hey.

BILL

Come on, April; knock it off. (*He sits at the switchboard.*)

APRIL

Bill, baby, you know what your trouble is? You've got Paul Grangeritis. You've not got the conviction of your passions.

JAMIE

April? What time is it?

APRIL

It's a quarter after— (*Looks at* BILL.)

BILL

(*A glance at the clock.*)

Twelve-thirty. Nearly.

APRIL

She probably got stopped on account of the license.

BILL

(*Under his breath*)

Sure she did.

(*To* MILLIE, *who is retiring*)

Millie, you want a wake-up call?

MILLIE

(*Almost laughing*)

Oh—no point in—unless you just feel like talking. Good night, everyone.

MR. MORSE
Paul Granger is an old fool!

MILLIE
Did you know him, Mr. Morse? Oh, God . . . I felt one of us should . . . remember him.

MR. MORSE
He's an old fool.

APRIL
(*Turning on the radio.*)
You tell 'em, baby.

BILL
Try to sleep this time.

MILLIE
(*Going off.*)
Well, if it happens . . .

APRIL
(*To* JAMIE *as the song comes on the radio*)
Come on, Jamie. Off your butt. Come on; dance with me. This may be your shining hour.

JAMIE
No, come on.

BILL
She's just teasing you.

APRIL
Hell I am.

JAMIE
I don't feel like it.

APRIL
You eaten anything today?
(*He nods.*)
What? Some health-nut crap?

JAMIE
Bacon and eggs and a hamburger.

APRIL
What kind of health food is that?

JAMIE
There's no health-food place close enough.

APRIL
Come on; you're so shy, if someone doesn't put a light under your tail, you're not going to have passions to need convictions for.
(JAMIE *walks uncertainly to* APRIL.)
(*A pizza* DELIVERY BOY *enters.*)

DELIVERY BOY
Somebody order a pizza here?

BILL
April?

APRIL
(*Without looking at him; taking the check.*)
Take it up to the second-floor john.

BILL
Second floor, turn right. The door at the end of the hall.
(DELIVERY BOY *goes.*)

JAMIE
I don't know how.

APRIL

Nobody knows how. What does it matter; the important thing is to *move*. Come on; all your blood's in your tail.

BILL

It's twelve-thirty; he's been up all day; he doesn't want to dance.

APRIL

Sure he does.

JAMIE

Tell me how.

APRIL

Come on, they're gonna tear up the dance floor in a minute; the bulldozers are barking at the door. Turn it up, Bill, or I'll break your arm.

(*He turns it up a little.*)

Turn it up!

(*More.*)

(APRIL *and* JAMIE *latch arms, go one way, then back. She joins in singing with the radio, and as the lights fade and they turn back, circling the other way, he joins in as well.* BILL *stares off, then smiles at them.* MR. MORSE *sips the drink and watches on.*)